2020

Wiley
CPAexcel®
EXAM REVIEW
FOCUS NOTES

Wiley

2020

CPAexcel®
EXAM REVIEW
FOCUS NOTES

AUDITING AND ATTESTATION

WILEY

CONTENTS

v

Contents  **vi**

Contents   vii

Contents

Contents

Contents   **x**

PREFACE

This publication is a comprehensive yet simplified study program. It provides a review of the basic skills and concepts tested on the CPA exam and teaches important strategies to take the exam faster and more accurately. This tool allows you to take control of the CPA exam.

This simplified and focused approach to studying for the CPA exam can be used:

- As a handy and convenient reference manual
- To solve exam questions
- To reinforce material being studied

Included is critical information necessary to obtain a passing score on the CPA exam in a concise and easy-to-use format. Due to the wide variety of information covered on the exam, a number of techniques are included:

- Acronyms and mnemonics to help you learn and remember a variety of rules and checklists
- Formulas and equations that simplify complex calculations required on the exam
- Simplified outlines of key concepts without the details that encumber or distract from learning the essential elements

- Techniques that can be applied to problem solving or essay writing, such as preparing a multiple-step income statement, determining who will prevail in a legal conflict, or developing an audit program
- Pro forma statements, reports, and schedules that make it easy to prepare these items by simply filling in the blanks
- Proven techniques to help you become a smarter, sharper, and more accurate test taker

This publication may also be useful to university students enrolled in Intermediate, Advanced, and Cost Accounting classes; Auditing, Business Law, and Federal Income Tax classes; or Economics and Finance Classes.

PROFESSIONAL RESPONSIBILITIES

Financial Statements, an Audit, and Audited Financial Statements

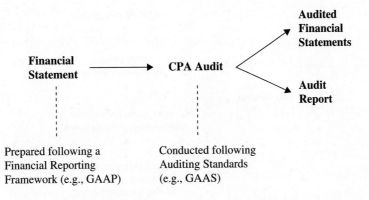

Financial Statement → CPA Audit → Audited Financial Statements / Audit Report

Prepared following a Financial Reporting Framework (e.g., GAAP)

Conducted following Auditing Standards (e.g., GAAS)

DIAGRAM OF AN AUDIT

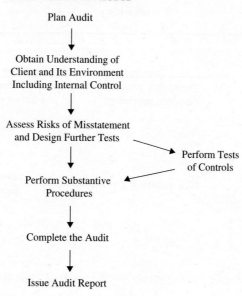

Plan Audit

↓

Obtain Understanding of
Client and Its Environment
Including Internal Control

↓

Assess Risks of Misstatement
and Design Further Tests

→ Perform Tests
of Controls

Perform Substantive
Procedures

↓

Complete the Audit

↓

Issue Audit Report

Focus on

Professional Responsibilities

2

Principles Underlying an Audit

- **Purpose of audit**—Provide an opinion.
- **Premise of audit**—Management has responsibility for preparing financial statements and providing auditor with all needed information.
- **Personal responsibilities of auditor**—Competence, follow ethical requirements, maintain professional skepticism.
- **Auditor actions in audit**— Plan and perform procedures to obtain reasonable assurance about whether financial statements are free from material misstatements.
- **Reporting results of an audit**—Written report with an opinion, or a statement that an opinion cannot be obtained.

Auditing Standard Requirement Categories

- **Unconditional requirement**—The auditor must comply with the requirement in all cases in which the circumstances exist. Auditing standards use the words *must*, *shall*, or *is required* to indicate an unconditional requirement.

- **Presumptively mandatory requirement**—Similarly, the auditor must comply with the requirement, but, in rare circumstances, the auditor may depart from such a requirement. In such circumstances, the auditor documents the departure, the justification for the departure, and how the alternative procedures performed in the circumstances were sufficient. Auditing standards use the word *should* to indicate a presumptively mandatory requirement.

Note: The PCAOB includes a third level, **Responsibility to Consider**, in which the auditor has the responsibility to consider identified actions/procedures and implement those matters exercising the appropriate professional judgment in the circumstances. Terms such as *may*, *might*, or *could* indicate a responsibility to consider.

Code of Professional Conduct

Sections

- Preface: applicable to all members
- Part 1: applicable to members in public practice
- Part 2: applicable to members in business
- Part 3: applicable to other members (associate, affiliate, and international associate members, retired and unemployed members)

Structure

- Principles (6 general statements)
- Rules of conduct (10 overall standards)
- Interpretations of the rules
- Other guidance (e.g., state CPA society, state board of accountancy, SEC, PCAOB, GAO, DOL, tax authorities)

Code of Professional Conduct (continued)

Principles

1. Responsibilities
2. Public Interest
3. Integrity
4. Objectivity and Independence
5. Due Care
6. Scope and Nature of Services

Rules and Applicability

Rules	Public Practice	Business	Other
Integrity and Objectivity	X	X	
Independence	X		
General Standards	X	X	
Compliance with Standards	X	X	
Accounting Principles	X	X	
Acts Discreditable	X	X	X
Fees and Other Types of Remuneration	X		
Advertising and Other Forms of Solicitation	X		
Confidential Client Information	X		
Form of Organization and Name	X		

Conceptual Frameworks

Code includes three conceptual frameworks for situations not explicitly addressed by a Rule.

1. **Members in public practice**—one independence conceptual framework and one general conceptual framework to address issues other than independence.
2. **Members in business**—a general conceptual framework.
3. All frameworks use an approach of considering seriousness of threats and whether safeguards reduce the risk to an acceptable level.

Threats and Safeguards Considered by Conceptual Frameworks

Threats

- Adverse interest
- Advocacy
- Familiarity
- Management participation (for public practice members only)
- Self-interest
- Self-review
- Undue influence

Safeguards

- Created by the profession, legislation, or regulation
- Implemented by the client
- Implemented by the CPA firm

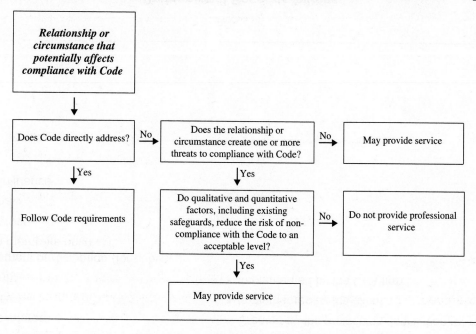

Relationship or circumstance that potentially affects compliance with Code

↓

Does Code directly address? — No → Does the relationship or circumstance create one or more threats to compliance with Code? — No → May provide service

↓ Yes

Follow Code requirements

↓ Yes

Do qualitative and quantitative factors, including existing safeguards, reduce the risk of non-compliance with the Code to an acceptable level? — No → Do not provide professional service

↓ Yes

May provide service

Independence Rule

- Only applies to members in public practice and their attest clients
- The concept of a **covered member** is important because, in general, covered members must be independent for the firm to retain its independence. Covered members include:
    - Members of attest engagement team
    - Person who may influence attest engagement (e.g., partner who supervises the partner in charge of the engagement)
    - All partners and partner equivalents in the office in which the lead attest partner practices
    - Certain partners, partner equivalents, and managers who perform nonattest services to the client (10-hour NAS providers)
    - The firm, including its benefit plans
    - Entities controlled by any of the above

Independence Requirements for all Partners and Staff

1. No partner or professional employee (or their immediate family members) or group acting together may own more than 5% of attest client's equity securities.
2. No partner or professional employee may be director, officer, employee, etc., of the client.
3. CPAs previously employed by a client, but now employed by CPA firm, must not be involved with the audit of any period during which they were employed by that client.

If any of the above situations occur, the CPA firm's independence is impaired and it may not provide attest services to that client.

Additional Independence Requirements for Covered Members—Financial

Financial relationships that *impair the independence of both the member and the firm* include:

(1) All direct financial interests (e.g., stock or debt investment in attest client)

(2) Material indirect financial interests (e.g., investment in a mutual fund heavily invested in the attest client)

(3) A material joint closely held investment held with an attest client (or one of the client's officers or directors, or any owner with significant influence over the attest client)

Additional Independence Requirements for Covered Members—Family

Interests of relatives and friends

(1) *Immediate family* (spouse, spousal equivalent, dependents)—same requirements as covered member, with limited exceptions.

(2) *Close relatives* (e.g., parents, siblings, or nondependent children)—overall, CPA firm independence is impaired if close relative has (a) a key position with the client, or (b) a material financial interest in the client of which the accountant has knowledge.

(3) *Other considerations for all relatives and friends*. Independence is only impaired when a reasonable person aware of the facts would conclude there is an unacceptable risk.

Examples of Activities that Impair Independence

- Supervising client's personnel
- Signing client's checks
- Acting as client's stock transfer agent
- Accepting gifts from client in violation of member or client policies

Independence—Unpaid Fees

- Unpaid fees may impair independence
  - May not extend beyond one year
  - Audit may be performed, but report may not be issued until prior year fees paid

Independence—Auditor on Engagement Considers or Takes Employment with Audit Client

- Individual must inform the audit firm when seeking or discussing potential employment with client.
- Individual's independence impaired (should be taken off job) until employment by client is no longer being considered by that individual.
- Once individual accepts employment with audit client, the audit firm should consider the need to modify the audit plan or change members of the audit.
- If a former partner or professional employee joins the client in a key position within a year after leaving the firm and has significant interaction with the audit team, a member of the audit firm with no connection to the audit must review the engagement to ensure it takes into account independence issues.

Independence—Nonattest Services

- May provide advice, research materials, and recommendations
- Client must accept responsibility for making all decisions
- Specific client personnel must be designated to oversee services
- Client must be responsible for establishing and maintaining all internal controls and may not "outsource" such services to the auditor
- An understanding of the objectives of the engagement and client responsibilities must be documented prior to performing the nonattest services for an attest client
- A conflict of interest may exist if member performing a service and the member/ member's firm has a relationship that could in the member's judgment be viewed as impairing the member's objectivity. For example,
  - Suggest that the client invest in a business in which he or she has a financial interest.
  - Provide tax services for several members of a family who may have opposing interests.
  - Have a significant financial interest or influence with a major competitor of a client.

Integrity and Objectivity—Members in Business

A member shall maintain objectivity and integrity, shall be free of conflicts of interest, and shall not knowingly misrepresent facts or subordinate his or her judgment to others.

- Misrepresentation of facts: Member is forbidden to knowingly (or let someone else)
    - Make materially false and misleading entries
    - Fail to correct financial statements or records that are materially false and misleading
    - Sign a document containing materially false and misleading information
- Obligations of a member to his or her employer's external accountant
    - Must be candid and not knowingly misrepresent facts or knowingly fail to disclose material facts
- Responsibilities in presenting information
    - In accordance with relevant reporting framework, when applicable
    - In a manner that does not attempt to or is not misleading, including significant omissions

Responsibilities to Clients

A member in public practice shall not

- Disclose any confidential client information without the specific consent of the client
- Accept a contingent fee for
  - An audit or review of a financial statement
  - A compilation of a financial statement
  - An examination of prospective financial information
- Prepare an original or amended tax return or claim for a tax refund for a contingent fee for any client

A CPA must maintain client information as confidential. May disclose client information

- To comply with a subpoena
- To cooperate with a quality control review
- When required by law to inform public authorities of violations

Other Responsibilities and Practices

A CPA should not perform acts discreditable to the profession, such as

- Retaining client records
- Understating anticipated fees for services
- Accepting a commission in relation to an attest client
- Practice under a misleading name

A CPA shall be competent.

- Agreeing to perform professional services implies that the member has the necessary competence to complete those professional services but is not infallible
- Involves both the technical qualifications of the member and staff and the ability to supervise and evaluate the quality of the work performed
- If the member does not have the necessary competence, may perform additional research or consult with others
- But if cannot attain competence, should recommend client seek help from someone else

Quality Control

CPA firms should establish quality controls to ensure compliance with professional standards.

Nature and extent of quality control policies and procedures will depend on

- Size of firm and number of offices
- Knowledge and experience of personnel and authority allowed to personnel
- Nature and complexity of firm's practice
- Cost-benefit considerations

Quality Control Elements

- Leadership responsibilities for quality within the firm
- Relevant ethical requirements
- Acceptance and continuance of client relationships and specific engagements
- Human resources
- Engagement performance
- Monitoring

Tax Preparer

Actions by an accountant preparing a client's tax return can result in penalties for

- Not providing client with copy of return
- Failing to sign return as a preparer
- Endorsing and cashing client's refund check
- Failing to file a timely return
- Not advising client of tax elections
- Neglecting evaluation of joint versus separate returns

A CPA performing tax services

- May not recommend a tax position that lacks merit
- Must make a reasonable effort to answer applicable questions on the return
- May rely on client information when preparing the return
- Must make reasonable inquiries about questionable or incomplete information
- May use estimates

Standards for Consulting Services

When performing consulting services, a CPA must adhere to certain general standards

- Professional competence
- Due professional care
- Planning and supervision
- Obtaining sufficient relevant data

GAO—GAGAS Ethical Principles

Apply to auditors of government entities and entities receiving government awards

GAGAS requires independence and compliance with key ethical principles

- The public interest
- Integrity
- Objectivity
- Proper use of government information, resources, and positions, and
- Professional behavior

Department of Labor Independence Requirements for Employee Benefit Plans

An accountant is not independent with respect to the plan if he/she

- Has direct financial interest or any material indirect financial interest in the plan or plan sponsor
- Is a promoter, underwriter, investment advisor, voting trustee, director, officer, or employee of the plan or plan sponsor
- Maintains financial records for the employee benefit plan

ASSESSING RISK AND DEVELOPING A PLANNED RESPONSE

Financial Statement Assertions

- Management's responsibility
- Assertions themselves

Transaction Classes	Account Balances	Disclosures
Occurrence	Existence	Occurrence and rights and obligations
	Rights and obligations	
Completeness	Completeness	Completeness
Accuracy	Valuation and allocation	Accuracy and valuation
Cutoff		
Classification		Classification and understandability

Audit Risk (AR)

AR is risk that material errors or fraud exist resulting in an inappropriate audit report

- Auditor uses judgment in establishing acceptable level of AR
- Lower acceptable level of AR achieved through obtaining more audit evidence

AR at the assertion level consists of inherent risk (IR), control risk (CR), and detection risk (DR)

IR acknowledges that certain items are more susceptible to risk

- May be due to complexity of transactions or calculations, ease of theft, or lack of available objective information
- IR is beyond control of auditor and generally beyond control of entity

CR acknowledges that misstatements may not be prevented or detected by entity's internal control

- Entity's internal control may be poorly designed or poorly executed
- CR is beyond control of auditor but within control of entity

The combination of IR and CR is referred to as the *risk of material misstatement*—these risks may be assessed separately, or in combination.

Audit Risk (continued)

DR acknowledges that auditor may not detect material misstatement

- Auditor may not properly plan or perform audit procedures
- DR is within control of auditor

Audit Risk = Risk of Material Misstatement * Risk Auditor Fails to Detect Misstatements

Audit Risk = Inherent Risk * Control Risk * Detection Risk

Components of Audit Risk

	Increases risk	Decreases risk
Inherent risk	Declining industry Lack of working capital High rate of obsolescence Complex calculations	More profitable than industry average Low management turnover Low estimation uncertainty
Control risk	Ineffective internal controls Weak management oversight	Effective internal control Strong management oversight
Detection risk	Decrease substantive testing Perform tests early in year	Increase extent of substantive procedures Select more effective tests Perform tests near year-end

Applying Audit Risk Model

$$AR = IR \times CR \times DR$$

To apply model

Establish acceptable level of audit risk

Assess inherent risk based on internal and external factors

Establish planned assessed level of control risk based on inquiries and other risk assessment procedures

- May set control risk at maximum level
- If control risk set below maximum, must perform tests of controls to verify assessment

Conceptually (or actually) one computes necessary level of detection risk

$$DR = AR \div (IR \times CR)$$

Determine if planned nature, timing, and extent of substantive tests are adequate to provide appropriate level of detection risk

Materiality

Magnitude of omission or misstatement that makes it probable that the judgment of a reasonable person relying on the information could have been changed or influenced by the omission or misstatement

Recognizes relative importance of items to fair presentation of financial statements

- Items may be material due to high dollar amount (Quantitative)
- Items may be material due to nonmonetary significance (Qualitative)

Determining materiality

- Auditors should determine materiality for financial statements as a whole
- Also, particular transactions, accounts, or disclosures may require lower levels

Materiality (continued)

Materiality is matter of professional judgment

- Must plan audit to obtain reasonable assurance that financial statements are not misstated
- Misstatements could be material individually or collectively
- Materiality measurement based on smallest aggregate level
- Performance materiality, ordinarily smaller than materiality, is used to determine that small misstatements do not total a material amount.

Evaluation of Misstatements

Misstatements should not just be evaluated quantitatively, but qualitatively, such as misstatements that

1) Affect trends of profitability.
2) Change losses into income.
3) Affect segment information.
4) Affect compliance with legal and contractual requirements.

Misstatements in a sample are likely to indicate greater misstatement in the population as a whole. The use of estimates in accounting increases the risk of material misstatements.

Consideration of Fraud in a Financial Statement Audit

Prevention and detection of fraud are management's responsibility

- Auditor provides reasonable assurance that financial statements are not materially misstated
- Providing absolute assurance is impossible due to inherent limitations of the audit, including (1) the nature of financial reporting, (2) the nature of audit procedures and (3) the need to conduct audit within a reasonable time period at a reasonable cost

Types of Fraud

Two types of fraud can result in material misstatement of financial statements

1) Fraudulent financial reporting—intentional misstatements or omissions
2) Misappropriations of assets (defalcations)—embezzlement, stealing, or misuse of funds

Fraud most often committed when there is

- Pressure or incentive
- Opportunity
- Rationalization (individual justifies the act to self)

Focus on
Assessing Risk and Developing a Planned Response

Steps in Consideration of Fraud

- Staff discussion of the risk of material misstatement
- Obtain information needed to identify risks of material misstatement
- Identify risks that may result in a material misstatement due to fraud
- Assess the identified risks after considering programs and controls
- Respond to the results of the assessment
- Evaluate audit evidence
- Communicate about fraud
- Document consideration of fraud

Throughout the engagement, the audit team should exercise **professional skepticism** regarding the possibility of fraud. Know that professional skepticism includes a questioning mind, being alert to conditions that may indicate fraud or error, and a critical assessment of audit evidence.

Fraud Risk Factors Overall

- Existence of certain factors leads auditor to conclude high risk of **fraudulent financial reporting** and/or **misappropriation of assets**
- Existence of a risk factor may lead the auditor to modify the scope of procedures (if the audit plan does not adequately address the risk).
- Skim specific factors quickly.

Fraud Risk Factors Overall (continued)

Fraudulent Financial Reporting

Management characteristics

- Compensation tied to aggressive results
- Excessive interest in stock prices and earnings
- Commitments made to analysts regarding achieving unrealistic forecasts
- Pursuit of minimizing earnings for tax purposes

Management's attitude toward internal control

- Management dominated by single person or small group
- Controls not adequately monitored
- Known weaknesses not corrected timely
- Unrealistic goals set for operating personnel
- Use of ineffective accounting, technology, or internal audit staff

Fraud Risk Factors Overall (continued)

Fraudulent Financial Reporting (continued)

Other management-related factors

- High turnover
- Strained relationship with auditor

Industry conditions

- New accounting rules or requirements impairing profitability
- High degree of competition
- Declining industry
- Volatile industry

Fraud Risk Factors Overall (continued)

Fraudulent Financial Reporting (continued)

Operating characteristics and financial instability of entity

- Negative cash flows
- Need for capital
- Use of estimates that are unusually subjective or subject to change
- Related-party transactions outside the ordinary course of business
- Significant or unusual transactions near year-end
- Overly complex structure
- Unusual growth or profitability
- Vulnerable to changes in interest rates
- Difficult debt covenants
- Overly aggressive incentive programs
- Threat of bankruptcy, foreclosure, or takeover
- Pending transaction that will be adversely affected by poor results

Fraud Risk Factors Overall (continued)

Misappropriation of Assets

Characteristics indicating lack of adequate control over susceptible assets

- Operations not subject to proper oversight
- Inadequate screening of applicants for positions with access to assets
- Inadequate recordkeeping
- Insufficient segregation of duties with lack of independent checks
- Inappropriate system for authorizing and approving transactions
- Inadequate physical safeguards over assets
- Untimely or inappropriate documentation of transactions
- No requirement for vacations among employees performing key functions

General Fraud Risk

Other factors increase general risk of material misstatement of financial statements due to fraud

- Low employee morale
- Employees financially stressed
- Adverse relationship between employees and management or entity

Assessing Risk of Fraud

Risk of material misstatement due to fraud part of audit risk

- Auditor must consider existence of risk factors when designing audit procedures
- Risk factors not necessarily indicative of existence of fraud
- Factors are considered individually and collectively

Auditor should make inquiries of management regarding

- Management's understanding of risk of fraud in entity
- Management's knowledge of fraud

Auditor may become aware of risk factors when

- Deciding on acceptance of the engagement
- Planning the engagement
- Obtaining an understanding of internal control
- Performing fieldwork

Effects of Fraud Assessment

Upon assessment of risk of fraud, auditor may

- Determine planned audit procedures are sufficient or
- Decide to modify planned procedures

Modifications may include

- Applying greater degree of skepticism
- Assigning higher level and/or more experienced personnel to engagement
- Evaluating management's accounting decisions more carefully

When modification not practical, auditor may withdraw from engagement

Fraud-Related Documentation

Assessment of risk of material misstatement due to fraud in planning engagement should be documented, including

- Staff discussion
- Risk factors identified
- Auditor's response to risk factors
- Further response indicated by detection of risk factors during audit

Actions Resulting from Evidence of Fraud

Upon detecting evidence of fraud, auditor should

- Notify appropriate level of management
- Inform audit committee whenever senior management is involved or whenever material fraud is committed by anyone within the organization
- Disclose to third parties only to comply with legal or regulatory requirements, in response to inquiries of a successor auditor, in response to a subpoena, or in accordance with requirements for audits of entities receiving governmental financial assistance

Laws and Regulations—Responsibility to Detect and Report Illegal Acts

Illegal acts may have a direct effect on financial statements or only an indirect effect

Responsibility:

Direct—Responsibility same as for errors and fraud (obtain reasonable assurance of detection of material misstatements).

Other—An audit in accordance with GAAS does not include audit procedures specially designed to detect illegal acts not having a material and direct effect on financial statement amounts and disclosures. However, when procedures applied for other purposes identify possible illegal acts, the auditor should apply audit procedures to determine whether an illegal act has occurred.

Laws and Regulations—Responsibility to Detect and Report Illegal Acts (continued)

When misstatement that indicates possibility of illegal acts is either material or materiality cannot be determined

- Discuss with appropriate level of management
- Attempt to obtain additional evidence
- Suggest, perhaps, that client see attorney
- Consider withdrawing from engagement

Circumstances may require modification of opinion

- Qualified or adverse opinion, depending on materiality, if illegal act with material effect on financial statements not properly reported or disclosed
- Disclaimer if client prevents auditor from obtaining sufficient evidence to evaluate occurrence

Refusal by client to accept a modified opinion may result in withdrawal from the engagement

Summary of Assurance Provided by Auditor

	Not material	Material
Errors	No assurance	Reasonable assurance
Fraud	No assurance	Reasonable assurance
Illegal acts with direct effect on financial statements	No assurance	Reasonable assurance
Other illegal acts (those with an indirect effect on financial statements)	No assurance	No assurance

Audit Planning: Communication with Predecessor Auditor

Successor must make inquiries of predecessor auditor before accepting engagement

- Successor initiates communication
- Requires permission of client
- Consider implications of client's refusal

Nature of inquiries

- Disagreements with management about audit procedures or accounting principles
- Communication with audit committee about fraud, illegal acts, or internal control
- Reason for change in auditor
- Integrity of management

Audit Planning: Engagement Letter

Includes clear understanding of nature of services and responsibility assumed

Understanding should be written and include

- **O**bjectives of engagement
- **R**esponsibilities of management
- **A**uditor's responsibilities
- **L**imitations of engagement

Understanding will also indicate

- **F**inancial records and information will be made available
- **I**ndication of compliance with applicable laws and regulations
- **L**etter of representations at conclusion of fieldwork
- **E**stablishment and maintenance of internal control
- **S**tatements are the responsibility of management

Audit Planning: Engagement Letter (continued)

An engagement letter may also address

- Fees to be charged by the auditor
- Immaterial errors or fraud not expected to be found by audit
- Reasonable assurance provided that statements are not materially misstated
- Material misstatements may not be detected

Planning Considerations

Audit planning—developing strategy for scope and conduct of audit based on

- Size and complexity of entity
- Auditor's experience with entity
- Auditor's knowledge of entity's business
- Entity's accounting policies
- Materiality levels
- Audit risk and planned assessed level of control risk
- Entity's business environment
- Methods of processing accounting information
- Items on financial statements prone to adjustment
- Conditions affecting audit tests
- Reports to be issued

Audit Planning Procedures

- Determine involvement of consultants, specialists, and internal auditors
- Read current year's interim financial statements
- Coordinate assistance of entity personnel
- Discuss with firm personnel responsible for nonaudit services matters affecting the audit
- Review correspondence files, prior year's working papers, permanent files, financial statements, and auditor's report
- Inquire about current business developments affecting entity
- Discuss type, scope, and timing of audit with management, board of directors, or audit committee
- Consider effects of recent pronouncements
- Establish timing of audit work
- Establish and coordinate staffing
- Compare financial statements to anticipated results
- Perform analytical procedures to identify risk areas
- Assess materiality and audit risk

Obtaining an Understanding of the Client and Its Environment

Auditors perform *risk assessment procedures,* including

- Inquiries of management and others within the entity
- Analytical procedures
- Observation and inspection
- Review of information obtained in prior periods

Auditors may also consider information obtained from others outside the entity, e.g., legal counsel, valuation experts, analysts' reports, trade journals.

Specialists

Auditors may rely on the work of specialists to

- Value assets
- Determine the physical characteristics of inventories
- Determine amounts derived through specialized techniques
- Interpret technical requirements, regulations, or agreements

Before relying on the work of a specialist, the auditor should

- Evaluate the qualifications of the specialist
- Understand the nature of the work to be performed by the specialist
- Evaluate the relationship of the specialist to the client

Specialists (continued)

In evaluating the findings of the specialist, the auditor should

- Understand the methods used and assumptions made
- Test data provided to the specialist
- Evaluate whether the findings support the related assertions

The use of a specialist will not generally have an effect on the auditor's report

- The auditor may not refer to the specialist in an unmodified report.
- The auditor may decide to modify the opinion if the findings of the specialist do not corroborate the related assertions

The use of a specialist will only be referred to in the audit report if the findings of the specialist resulted in a modification of the report

Communication of Certain Information to Those Charged with Governance

The following matters should be communicated:

Audit responsibilities under GAAS

1. Responsibility to form and express an opinion
2. An audit does not relieve management or those charged with governance of their responsibilities

Planned scope and timing of the audit—An overview of the planned scope and timing of the audit; this may assist those charged with governance in understanding the consequences of the auditor's work for their oversight activities and the auditor to understand better the entity and its environment.

Communication of Certain Information to Those Charged with Governance (continued)

Significant findings from the audit

1. Qualitative aspects of the entity's significant accounting practices
2. Significant difficulties encountered during the audit
3. Uncorrected misstatements
4. Disagreements with management
5. Other findings or issues, e.g., GAGAS requirements
6. If those charged with governance are not involved in managing the entity, the following should also be communicated:
   - Material corrected misstatements resulting from audit
   - Auditor's view on management's consultations with other accountants
   - Representations requested from management
   - Significant issues discussed, or subject to correspondence with management

UNDERSTANDING INTERNAL CONTROL AND ASSESSING CONTROL RISK

Consideration of Internal Control

Consideration of internal control is necessary to determine nature, timing, and extent of substantive tests

Internal control is defined as a process—effected by an entity's board of directors, management, and other personnel—designed to provide reasonable assurance regarding the achievement of objectives in the following categories:

(a) Reliability of financial reporting,
(b) Effectiveness and efficiency of operations, and
(c) Compliance with applicable laws and regulations.

Related to the above is the safeguarding of assets.

Components of Internal Control

Internal control consists of five interrelated components

1. **C**ontrol Activities
2. **R**isk Assessment
3. **I**nformation and Communication
4. **M**onitoring
5. Control **E**nvironment

Control Activities

Control activities are policies and procedures that help ensure that management directives are followed

The auditor will be concerned about

- **P**erformance reviews—comparisons of actual performance to expectations
- **I**nformation processing—checks on accuracy, completeness, and authorization of transactions
- **P**hysical controls—safeguarding assets and controlling access to records
- **S**egregation of duties—reducing opportunities for one individual to commit errors and conceal them

*I say! These control activities are **pips***

Duties requiring segregation are

- **A**uthorization
- **R**ecording
- **C**ustody

ARC

Risk Assessment

Risk assessment addresses how the company identifies, analyzes, and manages risk

Risks relevant to preparation of financial statements are affected by internal and external events and circumstances

- Changes in operating environment
- New personnel
- New information systems
- Rapid growth
- New technology
- New lines, products, or activities
- Corporate restructuring
- Foreign operations
- Accounting pronouncements

Risk Assessment (continued)

Entity Risk Assessment versus Auditor Risk Assessment

Entity—designed to identify, analyze, and manage risks that affect entity's objectives

Auditor—involves assessment of inherent risk and control risk to evaluate likelihood of material misstatements occurring in financial statements

Information and Communication

Information and communication relate to the identification, capture, and exchange of information that enables individuals to carry out their responsibilities

Monitoring

Monitoring by management allows for evaluation as to whether internal control is operating as planned

Control Environment

The control environment sets the tone of the organization

Factors include

- **I**ntegrity and ethical values
- **C**ommitment to competence
- **H**uman resource policies and practices
- **A**ssignment of authority and responsibility
- **M**anagement's philosophy and operating style
- **B**oard of directors or audit committee participation
- **O**rganizational structure

Understanding Internal Control

Understanding internal control assists auditors in

- Identifying types of potential misstatements and factors that affect the risks of material misstatement
- Designing the nature, timing, and extent of further audit procedures

Obtaining an Understanding of Internal Control during Risk Assessment

Risk assessment procedures for internal control include

- Inquiries of management and others within the entity
- Observing the application of specific controls
- Inspecting documents and records
- Tracing transactions through the information system (walk-throughs)

Uses of internal control understanding obtained during risk assessment

- Identify types of potential misstatements
- Consider factors that affect the risk of material misstatement
- Design tests of controls and substantive procedures (*further procedures*)

Understanding the Design of Internal Control

An understanding of the design allows an auditor to assess how internal control is intended to function

The auditor must understand each of the five components to

- Identify types of potential misstatements
- Consider factors that affect the risk of material misstatement
- Design substantive tests

To accomplish this, the auditor must perform procedures that will provide knowledge of

- The design of controls for each of the five components as they relate to the financial statements
- Whether controls have been placed in operation and are being used by client

Understanding the Design of Internal Control (continued)

In addition to previous experience, the auditor may perform such procedures as

- Making inquiries of appropriate individuals
- Inspecting documents and records
- Observing activities

The auditor is not required to evaluate the effectiveness of controls unless reliance upon them is intended

The auditor is required to document the understanding of the entity's internal control

Common forms of documentation include

- A **memorandum**, describing the entity's internal control in narrative form
- A **flowchart**, diagramming internal control
- An **internal control questionnaire**, providing management's responses to questions about internal control
- A **decision table**

Understanding the Design of Internal Control (continued)

Flowcharts

Flowcharts diagram the design of internal control

Symbols used

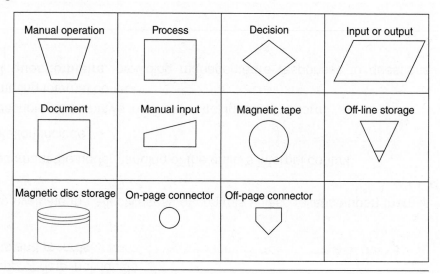

Manual operation	Process	Decision	Input or output
Document	Manual input	Magnetic tape	Off-line storage
Magnetic disc storage	On-page connector	Off-page connector	

Internal Control Questionnaire

Consists of series of questions asked of management

- Some questions designed to address objectives of internal control
- Other questions designed to address control activities intended to accomplish objectives

Questions designed to require *yes* or *no* answer

- *No* answer generally indicative of weakness in internal control
- Makes identification of weaknesses easier

Assessing Control Risk

Based on the understanding of the design of internal control, the auditor will establish a planned assessed level of control risk in relation to management's assertions

Control risk may be set at the maximum level for some or all assertions

- The auditor does not intend to rely on internal control in relation to those assertions
- Tests of controls will not be performed

Control risk may be set below maximum for some or all assertions

- The auditor must verify the effectiveness of internal control so that it can be relied upon
- Tests of controls will be performed

Assessing control risk below maximum involves two components

1) Identify controls that will prevent or detect material misstatements in specific assertions
2) Perform tests of control to evaluate the effectiveness of the controls identified

Tests of Controls

Tests of controls include

- **I**nquiry—Asking questions of appropriate personnel such as inquiring about the procedure followed when merchandise is received (insufficient alone as T of C)
- **I**nspection—Looking at documentary evidence such as inspecting paid invoices to make certain they have been cancelled to avoid double payment
- **O**bservation—Watching client employees as they perform such as observing employees receiving and recording purchases of merchandise to determine if there is proper segregation of duties
- **R**eperformance—Repeating procedures performed by client employees such as recounting inventories or recalculating invoice amounts

Know the four types of tests of controls

Tests of Controls (continued)

The auditor is required to evaluate the effectiveness of the design of internal control as part of obtaining an understanding.

Risk assessment procedures used to evaluate design include

- Inquire of appropriate personnel
- Inspect documents and reports
- Observe the application of specific controls

Tests of controls can then be used to evaluate the operating effectiveness of internal control in the desire to reduce the assessed level of control risk.

The auditor would

- Inquire of appropriate personnel (in combination with another procedure)
- Inspect documents and reports
- Observe the application of specific controls
- Reperform procedures performed by clients

Relationship of Control Risk to Tests of Controls, Detection Risk, and Substantive Procedures

	Control risk at maximum	Control risk below maximum
When appropriate	Internal control expected to be relatively ineffective Not cost effective to rely on internal control to reduce substantive procedures	Internal control expected to be relatively effective Cost effective to rely on internal control to reduce substantive procedures
Tests of controls	Not required	Required
Detection risk	Relatively low	Relatively high
Substantive procedures	Must be more effective	Can be less effective

Further Reducing the Assessed Level of Control Risk

Since many of the procedures used to understand the design of internal control are also used to support the assessed level of control risk

- Obtaining an understanding of internal control and supporting the assessed level of control risk are often done simultaneously
- The auditor may determine that additional tests of controls will provide evidence that will further reduce the assessed level of control risk

Concerning performing tests of controls, conceptually

- If their expected cost leads to a lower total expected audit cost than not performing them, they will be performed
- Tests of controls allow auditors to assess control risk below the maximum and to accept a higher level of detection risk

Documentation of Internal Control

The auditor should document

- The understanding of each of the IC components (control environment, risk assessment, control activities, information and communication, monitoring).
- The design of further audit procedures based on the understanding of IC (and other risk assessment procedures).
- The results of tests of controls (and other further audit procedures)
  - This will include the results of tests of controls as they provide evidence on operating effectiveness and may allow the auditor to assess control risk below the maximum.

Documentation of Internal Control (continued)

	Assess Control Risk at Below the Maximum Level	Assess Control Risk At the Maximum Level
Document understanding of entity's internal control?	Yes	Yes
Document basis for conclusion concerning control risk?	Yes	Yes
Perform tests of controls to determine effectiveness of policies and procedures?	Yes	No
Substantive procedures?	Yes, but limited if determined that the auditor can rely on internal control	Yes

Accounting Cycles

Cycles

- Revenue
- Purchases and spending
- Inventory and production
- Personnel and payroll
- Investing

Directional Testing

The concept of directional testing is particularly important relating to testing of the various cycles:

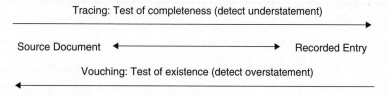

Tracing: Test of completeness (detect understatement)

Source Document   Recorded Entry

Vouching: Test of existence (detect overstatement)

In sentence form, the rules are

1. Tracing forward (source document to recorded entry) primarily tests completeness of recording and has a primary objective of detecting understatements.
2. Vouching (tracing backwards—recorded entry to source document) primarily tests existence and has a primary objective of detecting overstatements.

The Revenue Cycle

Controls Frequently Missing

Sales

(1) Credit granted by a credit department

(2) Sales orders and invoices prenumbered and controlled

(3) Sales returns are presented to receiving clerk who prepares a receiving report which supports prenumbered sales return credit memoranda

Accounts Receivable

(1) Subsidiary ledger reconciled to control ledger regularly

(2) Individual independent of receivable posting reviews statements before sending to customers

(3) Monthly statements sent to all customers

(4) Write-offs approved by management official independent of recordkeeping responsibility (e.g., the treasurer is appropriate)

The Revenue Cycle (continued)

Controls Frequently Missing

Cash Receipts

(1) Cash receipts received in mail listed by individuals with no recordkeeping responsibility
   (a) Cash goes to cashier
   (b) Remittance advices go to accounting
(2) Over-the-counter cash receipts controlled (cash register tapes)
(3) Cash deposited daily
(4) Employees handling cash are bonded
(5) **Lockbox,** a post office box controlled by the company's bank at which cash remittances from customers are received. The bank collects customer remittances, immediately credits the cash to the company's bank account, and forwards the remittance advices to the company. A lockbox system is considered an extremely effective control because company employees have no access to cash and bank employees have no access to the company's accounting records.
(6) Bank reconciliation prepared by individuals independent of cash receipts recordkeeping

The Purchases and Spending Cycle

Controls Frequently Missing

Purchases

(1) Prenumbered purchase orders used
(2) Separate purchasing department makes purchases
(3) Purchasing personnel independent of receiving and recordkeeping
(4) Suppliers' monthly statements compared with recorded payables

Accounts Payable

(1) Accounts payable personnel independent of purchasing, receiving, and disbursements
(2) Clerical accuracy of vendors' invoices tested
(3) Purchase order, receiving report, and vendor's invoice matched

The Purchases and Spending Cycle (continued)

Controls Frequently Missing

Cash Disbursements

(1) Prenumbered checks with numbers properly accounted for

(2) Two signatures on large check amounts

(3) Checks signed only with appropriate support (purchase order, receiving report, vendor's invoice). Treasurer signs checks and mails them

(4) Support for checks canceled after payment

(5) Voided checks mutilated, retained, and accounted for

(6) Bank reconciliations prepared by individual independent of cash disbursements recordkeeping

(7) Physical control of unused checks

The Inventory and Production Cycle

Controls Frequently Missing

(1) Perpetual inventory records for large dollar items

(2) Prenumbered receiving reports prepared when inventory received; receiving reports accounted for

(3) Adequate standard cost system to cost inventory items

(4) Physical controls against theft

(5) Written inventory requisitions used

(6) Proper authorization of purchases and use of prenumbered purchase orders

The Personnel and Payroll Cycle

Controls Frequently Missing

(1) Segregate: Timekeeping

                      Payroll preparation

                      Personnel

                      Paycheck distribution

(2) Time clocks used where possible

(3) Job time tickets reconciled to time clock cards

(4) Time clock cards approved by supervisors (overtime and regular hours)

(5) Treasurer signs paychecks

(6) Unclaimed paychecks controlled by someone otherwise independent of the payroll function (locked up and eventually destroyed if not claimed). In cases in which employees are paid cash (as opposed to checks) unclaimed pay should be deposited into a special bank account.

(7) Personnel department promptly sends termination notices to the payroll department.

The Investing Cycle

Controls Frequently Missing

(1) Segregation of duties among the individuals authorizing purchases and sales of securities, maintaining custody of the securities, and maintaining the records of securities

(2) Use of an independent agent such as a stockbroker, bank, or trust company to maintain custody of securities

(3) Securities **not** in the custody of an independent agent maintained in a bank safe-deposit box under the joint control of the treasurer and one other company official; both individuals must be present to gain access

(4) Registration of securities in the name of the company

(5) Detailed records of all securities and related revenue from interest and dividends

(6) Periodic physical inspection of securities by individuals with no responsibility for the authorization, custody, or recordkeeping for investments

Other Considerations

- Communication of internal control related matters to those charged with governance
- Communication of certain additional information to those charged with governance
- Effects of an internal audit function
- Reports on processing of transactions by service organizations

Those Charged with Governance

This ordinarily is the client's audit committee.

The client's audit committee is part of the board of directors

- Directors that are not officers or employees
- Liaison between auditor and board of directors

Audit committee

- Oversees financial reporting and disclosure process
- Hires auditor
- Reviews audit plan
- Reviews results and financial statements
- Oversees adequacy of internal control

Auditor and audit committee agree on

- Timing, fees, and responsibilities of parties
- Overall audit plan

Communication of Internal Control Related Matters to Those Charged with Governance

Both significant deficiencies and material weaknesses should be communicated in writing.

Deficiency	Severity	Required Communication to Management and Those Charged with Governance?
Control Deficiency	Design or operation of control does not allow management or employees, in the normal course of performing their assigned functions, to prevent or detect and correct misstatements on a timely basis.	ASB: To management if deficiency merits management's attention; PCAOB: May communicate to management as part of IC audit
Significant Deficiency	Less severe than a material weakness, yet important enough to merit attention by those charged with governance.	Yes
Material Weakness	A reasonable possibility that a material misstatement will not be prevented, or detected and corrected on a timely basis.	Yes

Effect of an Internal Audit Function

Primary effects of internal auditors

- **Work of the Internal Audit (IA) Function**—IA "ordinary" work may be used since IA is a part of internal control.
- **Direct assistance from IA Function**—CPAs may use IA to perform audit procedures under direction, supervision, and review of the CPA.

CPAs must evaluate internal auditor

- Competence (e.g., education, experience, certification).
- Objectivity (e.g., organizational status and relevant policies and procedures support internal audit objectivity).
- Application of a systematic and disciplined approach.

Reports on Processing of Transactions by Service Organizations

- Address situations where the audit client utilizes a service organization, e.g., payroll processing
- Allows Type 2 Report on the system description and the design and operating effectiveness of controls to be used to support the understanding of internal control
- Provided that the service auditor's competence and independence are satisfactory
- May allow Type 2 Report as audit evidence to support lowered control risk assessment

PERFORMING FURTHER PROCEDURES AND OBTAINING EVIDENCE

Sufficient Appropriate Audit Evidence

Reliability of Audit Evidence

While generalizations are difficult and subject to exceptions, audit evidence is ordinarily more reliable when it is

- Obtained from knowledgeable independent sources *outside the client company* rather than nonindependent sources
- Generated internally through a system of *effective controls* rather than ineffective controls
- Obtained *directly* by the auditor rather than indirectly or by inference (e.g., observation of application of a control is more reliable than an inquiry to the client concerning the control)
- *Documentary* in form (paper, electronic, or other) rather than an oral representation
- Provided by *original documents* rather than copies or facsimiles

Nature, Timing, and Extent of Audit Evidence

Audit risk model used to determine acceptable level of detection risk

- Understanding of design of internal control used to assess level of control risk
- Assessed level of control risk, along with inherent risk, used in audit risk model to determine level of detection risk that will provide acceptable level of audit risk
- Resulting acceptable level of detection risk may be high—Less substantive procedures are required
- Resulting acceptable level of detection risk may be low—More substantive procedures are required

Nature, Timing, and Extent of Audit Evidence (continued)

	Lower Detection Risk	Higher Detection Risk
Scope of Substantive Procedures	Higher	Lower
Nature	More reliable audit evidence (often externally generated)	Less reliable audit evidence
Timing	Gather audit evidence after year-end	Gather a significant portion of audit evidence prior to year-end (interim)
Extent	Verify a larger number of transactions or components of the account balance	Verify a smaller number of transactions or components of the account balance

Timing of Audit Procedures

Audit procedures may be performed at interim dates

Substantive testing performed before the balance sheet date

- Increases the risk that misstatements existing at balance sheet date will not be detected
- Referred to as **incremental audit risk**
- Incremental audit risk increases as time between tests and year-end is greater

Before performing substantive tests on an interim date, the auditor should consider

- Effectiveness of internal control
- Changing business conditions that may affect management's judgment in remaining period
- Whether year-end balances of accounts being tested are reasonably predictable

Tests should be performed at year-end to cover the remaining period

Basic Types of Audit Procedures

- **Risk assessment procedures**—Used to obtain an understanding of the entity and its environment, including its internal control.
- **Tests of controls**—When necessary, or when the auditor has decided to do so, used to test the operating effectiveness of controls at the relevant assertion level.
- **Substantive procedures**—Used to detect material misstatements in transactions, account balances, and disclosures. Substantive procedures include substantive analytical procedures and test of details of account balances, transactions, and disclosures.

(Tests of controls and substantive procedures are referred to as *further audit procedures*)

Types of Substantive Procedures

Substantive procedures may be tests of details or analytical procedures

Tests of details are designed to corroborate or contradict specific management assertions

- Tests of details include inquiries, confirmation, comparison, observation, recalculation, and examination.
- The result of the test will be information that either agrees with or does not agree with information presented or disclosed in the financial statements.

Some information cannot be directly corroborated or contradicted (e.g., the allowance for doubtful accounts and other estimates):

- Analytical procedures provide evidence as to the reasonableness of management's assertions.
- Analytical procedures involve comparing information in the financial statements to expectations to evaluate the reasonableness of the financial statement amounts.
- Analytical procedures may involve financial and nonfinancial data.

Analytical Procedures

Analytical procedures (APs) involve comparing amounts recorded in the financial statements or ratios derived from those amounts to expectations

Expectations may be based on

- Prior financial information
- Budgeted, forecasted, or otherwise anticipated results
- Relationships among elements of the current period's financial statements
- Industry averages
- Relationship between financial and nonfinancial information

APs are used in various stages of the audit

- **Risk Assessment** (for planning)—Used to identify aspects of the entity of which the auditor was unaware and to assist in assessing the risks of material misstatement. (Required)

- **Substantive procedures**—Used to obtain relevant and reliable audit evidence to substantiate accounts for which overall comparisons are helpful. (Not required)

- **Near end of audit** (overall review)—Used to assess conclusions reached and evaluate overall financial statement presentation. (Required)

Analytical Procedures (continued)

APs Used for Risk Assessment

APs can be used in risk assessment to

- Enhance the auditor's understanding of the client's business and industry
- Enhance the auditor's understanding of transactions and events occurring since the previous audit
- Identify areas representing risks that are relevant to the audit

APs may help auditors to identify

- Unusual transactions and events
- Ratios and trends that might affect the financial statements, particularly those involving income statement accounts

APs assist auditor in planning the nature, timing, and extent of audit procedures

Analytical Procedures (continued)

APs Used in Substantive Testing

Depending upon the level of assurance needed in relation to a specific management assertion

- APs alone may be sufficient
- APs may be used in conjunction with tests of detail
- APs may not be appropriate

When applying APs to substantive testing

1) Evaluate nature of assertion to determine if APs are appropriate and if use of APs will be efficient and effective
2) Evaluate whether plausible relationship exists and whether relationship is predictable
3) Determine if information is available and evaluate reliability of available information

Analytical Procedures (continued)

4) Determine if expectation is sufficiently precise to provide meaningful conclusions

- When information is expected to precisely match anticipated information, differences can be very useful in identifying potential misstatements
- When information is not expected to precisely match anticipated information, differences may be result of variety of causes

5) Investigate and evaluate differences

APs Used near End of Audit

Used to evaluate conclusions drawn as a result of audit

Involves

- Reading financial statements and notes
- Considering adequacy of evidence gathered
- Considering unusual or unexpected items not previously identified

May result in determination that additional evidence is required

Analytical Procedures (continued)

Ratios Commonly Used in APs

1) Liquidity ratios

   Current ratio = Current assets ÷ Current liabilities

   Quick or acid test ratio = Quick or liquid assets ÷ Current liabilities

   Quick or liquid assets are cash and cash equivalents, current investments in marketable securities, and net accounts receivable

2) Activity ratios

   Accounts receivable turnover = Net credit sales ÷ Average net accounts receivable

   Inventory turnover = Cost of goods sold ÷ Average inventory

   Asset turnover = Net sales ÷ Average total assets

Analytical Procedures (continued)

3) Profitability ratios

Profit margin percentage = Net income ÷ Net Sales

Gross profit percentage = Gross profit ÷ Net Sales

4) Coverage ratios

Times interest earned = Income before interest and taxes ÷ Interest expense

Debt to equity percentage = Total liabilities ÷ Total stockholders' equity

Audit Data Analytics (ADAs)

Techniques used to analyze large data sets in an audit

- Aid in discovering patterns and identifying anomalies
- Used to extract useful information in data
- Includes analysis, modeling, and visualization

May be used for:

- Risk assessment
- Tests of control
- Substantive procedures
- Evaluating conclusions

Audit Data Analytics (ADAs) (continued)

Five-step approach to using ADAs:

1. Plan the ADA.
2. Access and prepare data for use (ETL—extract, transform, load).
3. Consider relevance and reliability of data used.
4. Perform ADAs.
5. Evaluate results.

ADAs on very large data sets often involve visualization graphics (e.g., charts, tables).

Issues Related to Substantive Testing

Accounting Estimates

Auditor responsible for reasonableness of estimates used in determining the amounts of elements of the financial statements

When evaluating reasonableness, the auditor concentrates on assumptions or factors

- Significant to the estimate
- Sensitive to variation
- Apparent deviations from historical patterns
- Subjective and susceptible to bias or misstatement

Accounting Estimates (continued)

The auditor should understand how management develops estimates and obtain satisfaction through

- Reviewing and testing the process used by management (recalculation)
- Developing an independent expectation of the estimate to compare to management's amount (analytical procedures)
- Review subsequent events or transactions prior to completing fieldwork to verify the estimate (comparison)

The auditor must gain an understanding of

- How management develops its fair value measurements and disclosures, including
  - The experience of the personnel involved in the measurements
  - The significant assumptions used to develop the estimates
  - The relevant market information used to develop these assumptions (e.g., stock price quotations and official commodity price indexes)

Accounting Estimates (continued)

- The procedures used to monitor changes in the assumptions and estimates
- The extent to which management used outside specialists to develop the estimates

- Procedures for estimating fair values in accordance with GAAP, including
  - Market price data
  - Discounted cash flow methods
  - Use of appraisals from qualified specialists

- Risks associated with the use of estimates that could result in misstatement, based on the number, significance, and subjectivity of assumptions used to make the estimates

Management Representations

The auditor must obtain written representations from management indicating

- **I**nformation and data were available to the auditor during the examination
- **R**esponsibility for the financial statements rests with management
- **E**rrors, fraud, and material litigation that are known at year-end have been communicated
- **S**ubsequent events that may affect carrying values have been communicated
- **P**lans of the company that may affect carrying values have been communicated
- **O**ral information provided to the auditor was accurate and complete
- **N**oncompliance with laws and regulations that are known at year-end have been communicated
- **D**isclosure of major transactions, events, or circumstances affecting the client at year-end has been made

Management Representations (continued)

Written representations of management are addressed to the auditor

- Dated as of the date of the auditor's report
- Generally signed by chief executive officer and chief financial officer

When management will not supply a written representation letter

- Constitutes a scope limitation
- Auditor precluded from issuing unqualified opinion
- May affect auditor's attitude toward other information supplied by management

Litigation, Claims and Assessments

Management is responsible for identifying, evaluating, and accounting for litigation, claims, and assessments (LC&A)

Management asserts that all LC&A have been appropriately considered and are properly reflected in the financial statements and related disclosures

The auditor obtains evidence relating to

- The existence of conditions indicating an uncertainty arising from LC&A
- The period in which the cause for the uncertainty occurred
- The probability of an unfavorable outcome
- The amount or range of potential loss

Litigation, Claims, and Assessments (continued)

The auditor's procedures will include

- Inquire of management policies and procedures for identifying, evaluating, and accounting for LC&A
- Obtain from management a description and evaluation of LC&A existing at the balance sheet date
- Examine documents, including correspondence and invoices from lawyers concerning LC&A
- Obtain written assurance from management that all unasserted claims that are probable of assertion have been disclosed
- Obtain letter from client's attorney regarding LC&A

Client sends letter to attorney requesting corroboration of information supplied by management regarding LC&A

Included in letter

- Identification of company and date of audit
- List prepared by management describing and evaluating pending or threatened LC&A

Litigation, Claims, and Assessments (continued)

- List prepared by management describing and evaluating unasserted claims and assessments management considers probable of assertion
- Request that lawyer furnish information regarding pending or threatened LC&A
- Request that lawyer comment on views differing from those of management related to LC&A
- Statement that lawyer will advise and consult with client regarding disclosure of unasserted possible claims or assessments
- Request that lawyer identify nature of and reasons for limitations on response to inquiry

The lawyer will respond with

- Description of pending LC&A including progress to date and intended actions
- Evaluation of probability of unfavorable outcome and estimate of range of loss
- Omissions, if any, of pending or threatened LC&A from list prepared by client

Lawyer's refusal to respond represents a scope limitation

Related Parties

Audit procedures should be performed to identify and evaluate the disclosure of related-party transactions

In performing the audit, transactions may come to the auditor's attention indicating the existence of related parties

- Borrowing or lending at no interest or at rates significantly different from market rates
- Sales of real estate at prices significantly different from appraised values
- Exchanges of similar property in nonmonetary transactions
- Loans with no scheduled terms

Procedures the auditor will apply include

- Examine minutes of board meetings
- Examine transactions with major customers, supplier, borrowers, and lenders for indications of relationship
- Examine large, unusual, or nonrecurring transactions at or near year-end
- Examine confirmations of loans receivable and payable for guarantees

Related Parties (continued)

If related-party transactions are identified, auditor should

- Obtain understanding of business purpose of transaction
- Examine invoices, agreements, and contracts
- Determine whether the directors have approved the transaction
- Evaluate whether related party relationships and transactions have been properly accounted for and disclosed

Subsequent Events

Subsequent events occur after the balance sheet date but before issuance of the financial statements

Subsequent events may relate to condition existing at balance sheet date

- Examples may include settlement of litigation or learning of the bankruptcy of a customer
- Effects of these events require adjustment to financial statements

Subsequent events may relate to condition not existing at balance sheet date

- Examples may include sale of securities or loss due to natural disaster
- Effects of these events do not require adjustments to financial statements
- May require disclosure

Subsequent Events (continued)

Procedures after the balance sheet date may include

- Comparing subsequent interim financial information to audited financial statements
- Making inquiries of management
- Investigating changes in long-term debt or equity
- Reading minutes of board meetings and stockholder meetings
- Making inquiries of legal counsel concerning litigation, claims, and assessments arising after year-end

Subsequent Discovery of Facts

After issuing report auditor may become aware of information that existed at balance sheet date

If facts would have affected report

- Auditor should determine if information is reliable
- Auditor should determine if users are still likely to be relying on report

Auditor should try to prevent further reliance on report

- Advise client to make appropriate disclosure to parties known to be relying on the report
- Client may issue revised financial statements
- Disclosure may be made in imminent subsequent financial statements

In case of refusal by client, notify board of directors of need to take appropriate steps

- May notify client that report should not be associated with financial statements
- May notify regulatory agencies that report should not be relied upon
- May notify each person known to be relying on report that it should not be relied on

Omitted Procedures

Auditor may determine that a substantive procedure considered necessary was not performed during the audit

- Other procedures may have compensated for omission
- Omitted procedure may impair ability to support opinion

If opinion affected, omitted procedure should then be applied

- Alternative procedures may be substituted
- If auditor becomes aware of previously unknown facts, rules for subsequent discovery of facts are applied

Audit Documentation

Working Papers

Working papers are documentation of work performed

- Demonstrate auditor's adherence to the professional standards
- Assist the auditor in conducting and supervising the audit

Working papers are maintained in permanent files and current files

Working Papers (continued)

Permanent files relate to the company and contain information with long-term significance

They are of ongoing interest in any period under audit and often include

- Debt agreements
- Pension contracts
- Articles of incorporation
- Flowcharts of internal control
- Bond indenture agreements
- Lease agreements
- Analyses of capital stock and stockholders' equity accounts

Working Papers (continued)

Current files relate specifically to the current period's audit

They often include

- Reconciliation of accounting records to financial statements or other information reported on
- Lead schedules reflecting major components of amounts in the financial statements
- Supporting schedules providing detail making up major components
- Documentation of substantive procedures performed providing evidence corroborating or contradicting management's assertions
- The attorney's letter and management's representation letter
- Audit programs

Working papers are the property of the auditor and should be maintained for the required period

Working papers may be in the form of electronic files

PCAOB Audit Requirement

For audits of public companies reporting to the SEC, audit documentation must include the preparation of an **engagement completion document.**

- This document must include all significant findings or issues arising from the engagement.
- All documentation necessary to understanding these findings must either be included in the engagement completion document or else must be cross-referenced to the working papers that provide such documentation.

AUDITING SPECIFIC ACCOUNTS

Using Management Assertions to Develop Audit Programs

For each management assertion, the auditor selects auditing procedures from a variety of procedures such as

- *Inspection of records or documents* (e.g., invoice for an equipment purchase transaction)
- *Inspection of tangible assets* (e.g., inventory items)
- *Observation* (e.g., observation of inventory count, observation of control activities)
- *Inquiry* (e.g., written inquiries and oral inquiries)
- *Confirmation* (e.g., accounts receivable)
- *Recalculation* (e.g., checking the mathematical accuracy of documents or records)
- *Reperformance* (e.g., reperforming the aging of accounts receivable)
- *Analytical procedures* (e.g., evaluating numbers for reasonableness, calculating ratios)

Test of Balances Approach versus Test of Transactions Approach

- Accounts can be audited using either a test of balances approach or a test of transactions approach.
- Basic difference in approaches:
  - Test of balances in essence audits entire account balance (effective for high turnover accounts)
  - Test of transactions approach emphasizes transactions occurring during the year (effective for low turnover accounts)

Test of Balances Approach

The test of balances approach is more appropriate when

- The number of transactions is relatively high
- The dollar amount per transaction is relatively low
- The acceptable level of detection risk is high

Accounts for which this approach is appropriate include cash, accounts receivable and sales, inventory, and accounts payable

This approach involves three steps

1) Identify the components that make up the account balance (e.g., individual account balances for accounts receivable)
2) Select the components to be verified
3) Verify the components through the use of substantive procedures

Test of Transactions Approach

The test of transactions approach is more appropriate when

- The number of transactions is relatively low
- The dollar amount per transaction is relatively high
- The acceptable level of detection risk is low

Accounts for which this approach is appropriate include long-term investments and investments in marketable securities; property, plant, and equipment; long-term debt; and equity

This approach involves five steps

1) Verify account's beginning balance from prior-year information (minimal work if audited)
2) Test transactions occurring during the current period through the use of substantive procedures
3) Verify resulting ending balance in account
4) Determine if ending balance is in need of adjustment due to impairment, change in market value, or other factor
5) Perform other procedures for management assertions not already addressed

Auditing Accounts

We will organize audit procedures about the following summary assertions:

- **E**—Existence—assets, liabilities, and equity interests exist, and recorded transactions and events have occurred.
- **R & O**—Rights and obligations—the company holds rights to the assets, and liabilities are the obligations of the company.
- **C**—Completeness—all assets, liabilities, equity interests, and transactions that should have been recorded have been recorded.
- **V**—Valuation and allocation—all transactions, assets, liabilities, and equity interests are included in the financial statements at proper amounts.

Auditing Cash

Various procedures used to audit cash

- Auditor ordinarily will desire high level of assurance in relation to cash
- Auditor will generally use a test of balances approach

AICPA Standard Bank Confirmation

- Form developed by AICPA used in all financial statement audits
- Provided to each bank in which client has or had accounts
- Requests information regarding balances, loans, and restrictions on cash balances

R & O—Management asserts that cash reported on balance sheet belongs to client

- Inquire of management if there are restrictions on cash
- Confirm with bank, using AICPA Standard Bank Confirmation, that there are no restrictions on cash such as compensating balances

Auditing Cash *(continued)*

V—Management asserts that cash is reported on balance sheet in correct amount

- Confirm balance per bank using AICPA Standard Bank Confirmation
- Compare amount on confirmation to amount on bank reconciliation
- Compare ending balance on bank reconciliation to schedule of cash balances
- Compare total amount from schedule of cash balances to amount reported on balance sheet
- Observe counts of cash on hand
- Recalculate amounts on bank reconciliation
- Examine interbank transfer schedule to verify absence of kiting

C—Management asserts that cash reported on balance sheet represents all of the company's cash and that all transactions involving cash were recorded in the appropriate period

- Confirm that reconciling items are reported in appropriate period using bank cutoff statement
- Compare deposits in transit on bank reconciliation to deposits reported in the cutoff statement
- Compare outstanding checks on bank reconciliation to checks cleared in the cutoff statement

Auditing Cash (continued)

E—Management asserts that cash reported on the balance sheet actually exists

- Confirm bank deposits using AICPA Standard Bank Confirmation
- Confirm certificates of deposit and other cash equivalents held by bank or others
- Observe cash on hand
- Examine certificates of deposit and other cash equivalents on hand

Auditing Accounts Receivable and Sales

A common tool used in auditing accounts receivable is the accounts receivable confirmation

- The auditor sends the confirmation to the client's customer
- The customer corroborates or contradicts the amount the client indicates is owed

Confirmations required unless

- Account balance immaterial,

- Confirmations ineffective, or

- Assessed RMM is low and other substantive procedures are adequate

Positive confirmations—require a response from the customer indicating agreement or disagreement with amount indicated by the client (sometimes amount claimed by the client is not provided to customer; this may be called a **blank confirmation)**

Negative confirmations—require a response only if customer disagrees with balance

Used when

- Relatively high number of accounts with relatively low balances

Auditing Accounts Receivable and Sales (continued)

- Acceptable detection risk is relatively high
- Customer is more likely to respond

R & O—Management asserts that company is entitled to the amounts reported as accounts receivable

- Inquire of management if accounts receivable have been pledged, assigned, or sold
- Examine loan agreements for indications of accounts receivable financing
- Examine minutes of meetings of board of directors for indications of accounts receivable financing

V—Management asserts that accounts receivable is reported at its net realizable value

- Inquire of management as to policies for collecting and writing off delinquent accounts
- Confirm balances in accounts receivable using positive or negative confirmations
- Compare amounts reported on confirmations to accounts receivable schedule
- Compare total of accounts receivable schedule to amount reported on balance sheet
- Recalculate balances of the allowance for uncollectible accounts and allowances for sales discounts and sales returns and allowances

Auditing Accounts Receivable and Sales (continued)

- Examine the aged analysis to determine if allowances are reasonable
- Examine subsequent collections and shipping documents for receivables for which positive confirmations were not returned
- Apply analytical procedures to determine if accounts receivable balance is reasonable in relation to sales and other factors

C—Management asserts that all amounts owed to the company resulting from sales on account are included in accounts receivable and that all transactions related to sales and accounts receivable were recorded in the appropriate period

- Compare shipping documents to amounts recorded as sales to determine if all sales were recorded
- Examine numerical sequence of prenumbered shipping documents and invoices to make certain that all numbers are accounted for
- Examine shipping logs and shipping documents for shipments at or near year-end to verify appropriate cutoff

Auditing Accounts Receivable and Sales (continued)

E—Management asserts that amounts reported as accounts receivable exist and reported sales transactions actually occurred

- Confirm amounts reported in accounts receivable using positive or negative confirmations
- Compare recorded sales to invoices and shipping documents to determine that goods were sold and shipped
- Compare deposits to dates receipts were recorded to verify absence of lapping
- Examine subsequent collections and shipping documents for receivables for which positive confirmations were not returned

Auditing Inventory

R & O—Management asserts that the company owns the inventory reported and that it has not been pledged as collateral for a loan

- Inquire of management if inventory is being held on consignment or has been pledged as security
- Examine loan agreements to determine if inventory is pledged as security
- Examine purchase invoices to verify that inventory is owned rather than held on consignment
- Examine minutes of directors' meetings for indications of inventory financing

V—Management asserts that inventory is properly reported using an appropriate inventory valuation method and at the lower of cost or market when appropriate

- Observe counts and perform test counts of inventory to verify accuracy
- Compare amounts resulting from test counts to amounts reported on inventory schedules
- Inquire as to the inventory valuation method in use
- Examine inventory schedules to verify proper application of inventory cost method
- Compare inventory costs to amounts on purchase invoices

Auditing Inventory (continued)

- For manufactured inventory: Examine cost sheets for proper handling of direct materials, direct labor, and application of overhead
- For manufactured inventory: Compare amounts from cost sheets to amounts reported for manufactured inventory
- Recalculate selected amounts and totals on inventory schedules using costs and quantities to verify accuracy
- Compare totals from inventory schedules to amounts reported on balance sheet
- Apply analytical procedures to determine if inventory is reasonable in relation to cost of sales and other related items

C—Management asserts that all inventory owned by the company is included in the reported balance and that all transactions related to inventory are recorded in the appropriate period

- Inquire of management as to inventories stored outside the entity
- Confirm inventories held by consignees, warehouses, and others outside the entity
- Compare amounts from test counts to inventory schedules

Auditing Inventory (continued)

- Compare totals of inventory schedules to amount reported on balance sheet
- Examine shipping documents for goods in transit to determine if appropriately included or excluded from inventory

E—Management asserts that all inventory that is reported in the financial statements actually exists

- Confirm inventories held by consignees, public warehouses, and others outside the entity
- Observe the counting of inventory
- Examine shipping documents for inventory in transit

Auditing Accounts Payable and Purchases

R & O—Management asserts that the company is obligated to pay accounts payable

- Compare amounts showing as payable to vendors' invoices, receiving reports, and purchase orders to verify that payables are for goods ordered and received
- Examine vendors' invoices, receiving reports, and purchase orders

V—Management asserts that accounts payable is reported at the amount that the company is obligated to pay

- Confirm amounts reported as payables with vendors
- Compare amounts reported as payables to vendors' invoices, receiving reports, and purchase orders
- Compare amount on schedule of accounts payable to amount reported on financial statements
- Recalculate totals of accounts payable schedule
- Apply analytical procedures to determine if relationships between accounts payable and purchases, inventory, cost of goods sold, and other items are reasonable

Auditing Accounts Payable and Purchases (continued)

C—Management asserts that all amounts owed to vendors for purchases on account are included in accounts payable and that all transactions related to accounts payable and purchases are reported in the appropriate period

- Confirm with vendors that balances are complete
- Confirm with vendors with zero balances to determine if amounts are owed
- Compare receiving reports to vendors' invoices and amounts recorded in accounts payable
- Examine payments made shortly after year-end to determine if goods or services were received before year-end

E—Management asserts that the obligation to pay accounts payable exists and that all purchase transactions did occur

- Confirm accounts payable with vendors
- Compare amounts reported in accounts payable to vendors' invoices, receiving reports, and purchase orders
- Examine payments after year-end to verify obligation existing at year-end

Auditing Investments and Investment Income

1) Verify account's beginning balance from prior-year information
   - Compare beginning balance in investment accounts to amounts reported on previous period's balance sheet (V)

2) Test transactions occurring during the current period through the use of substantive procedures
   - Inquire of management about acquisitions and disposals of investments during period (R & O, C, E)
   - Inquire of management about means of determining value of investments other than marketable securities (V)
   - Confirm purchases or sales where documents are not in evidence (R & O, C, E)
   - Compare amounts reported as investment income to amounts published in investment periodicals (V, C, E)
   - Compare amounts reported as investment income to amounts deposited (V, C, E)

Auditing Investments and Investment Income (continued)

- Compare amount recorded as cost of investment to documents from brokers, partnership agreements, and joint venture agreements (V)
- Recalculate amortization of discount or premium and verify proper recording (V)
- Recalculate gains and losses on sales based on documents from brokers or amounts deposited and carrying value of investment (V)
- Examine documents from brokers and canceled checks to verify acquisitions (R & O, V, E)
- Examine audited financial statements of investees accounted for under equity method to verify amount reported as income (V)
- Examine minutes of directors' meetings for indications of authorization of acquisitions and disposals of investments (C)
- Apply analytical procedures to verify reasonableness of amount reported as interest income (V, C)

3) Verify resulting ending balance in account
- Recalculate ending balance based on beginning balance and transactions during the period (V)

4) Determine if ending balance is in need of adjustment due to impairment, change in market value, or other factor

- Inquire of management if any long-term investments or investments in marketable securities classified as available for sale have experienced a nontemporary decline in value (V)

- Confirm investments held by brokers or other outside parties to verify they are still in existence and owned by the company (R & O, C, E)

- Compare carrying value of investments to market values to verify that investments are carried at lower of cost or market when appropriate (V)

- Examine stock certificates, bonds, partnership agreements, or joint venture agreements to verify that investments exist (E)

Auditing Property, Plant, and Equipment

1) Verify account's beginning balance from prior-year information
   - Compare beginning balance in property, plant, and equipment accounts to amounts reported on previous period's balance sheet (V)

2) Test transactions occurring during the current period through the use of substantive procedures
   - Inquire of management about acquisitions and disposals of property, plant, and equipment during period (R & O, C, E)
   - Inquire of management about methods, lives, and salvage values used to calculate depreciation (V)
   - Confirm purchases or sales where documents are not in evidence (R & O, C, E)
   - Compare amount recorded as cost of property, plant, and equipment to purchase documents and cancelled checks (V)
   - Recalculate costs to be capitalized for delivery, installation, or preparation of property, plant, and equipment for use (V, C)

Auditing Property, Plant, and Equipment (continued)

- Recalculate depreciation expense and verify proper recording (V)
- Recalculate gains and losses on sales based on amounts deposited and carrying value of property, plant, and equipment (V)
- Examine invoices and canceled checks to verify acquisitions (R & O, V, E)
- Examine minutes of directors' meetings for indications of authorization of acquisitions and disposals of property, plant, and equipment (C)

3) Verify resulting ending balance in account
- Recalculate ending balance based on beginning balance and transactions during the period (V)

4) Determine if ending balance is in need of adjustment due to impairment, change in market value, or other factor
- Inquire of management if any impairments have occurred affecting property, plant, and equipment (V)
- Examine property, plant, and equipment to verify that they exist (E)

Auditing Long-Term Debt and Interest Expense

1) Verify account's beginning balance from prior-year information
   - Compare beginning balance in long-term debt accounts to amounts reported on previous period's balance sheet (V)

2) Test transactions occurring during the current period through the use of substantive procedures
   - Inquire of management about issuance and retirements of long-term debt during period (R & O, C, E)
   - Compare amounts reported as interest expense to amounts disbursed (V, E)
   - Compare amount recorded as proceeds from issuance to confirmations from underwriters and amounts deposited (V, E)
   - Compare amounts reported in cash receipts journal to amounts recorded as initial carrying value of long-term debt (V, C)
   - Recalculate amortization of discount or premium and verify proper recording (V)
   - Recalculate gains and losses on early retirements (V)

Auditing Long-Term Debt and Interest Expense (continued)

- Examine documents from underwriters and trustees to verify issuances (R & O, V, E)
- Examine minutes of directors' meetings for indications of authorization of issuances and retirements of long-term debt (C)
- Apply analytical procedures to verify reasonableness of amount reported as interest expense (V, C)

3) Verify resulting ending balance in account
- Recalculate ending balance based on beginning balance and transactions during the period (V)

4) Determine if ending balance is in need of adjustment due to impairment, change in market value, or other factor
- Confirm obligations with trustees or other outside parties to verify there are no unrecorded liabilities (R & O, C, E)
- Confirm obligations with creditors to determine that they are the obligations of the company (R & O, E)
- Examine bond agreements and long-term notes to verify that long-term liabilities exist (E)

Auditing Equity

1) Verify account's beginning balance from prior-year information
   - Compare beginning balance in stockholders' equity accounts to amounts reported on previous period's balance sheet (V)

2) Test transactions occurring during the current period through the use of substantive procedures
   - Inquire of management about issuance and retirements of equity securities during period (R & O, C, E)
   - Compare amounts reported as dividends to amounts disbursed (V, E)
   - Compare amount recorded as proceeds from issuance to confirmations from underwriters and deposits (V, E)
   - Compare amounts reported in cash receipts journal to amounts recorded as proceeds from issuance of securities (V, C)

- Examine documents from underwriters and stock transfer agents to verify issuances and repurchases of stock (R & O, V, E)
- Verify changes in Accumulated Other Comprehensive Income amounts (V)
- Examine minutes of directors' meetings for indications of authorization of dividends and issuances and retirements of equity securities (C)

3) Verify resulting ending balance in account
   - Recalculate ending balance based on beginning balance and transactions during the period (V)

AUDIT SAMPLING

Sampling is used in both tests of controls and substantive testing.

- Nonstatistical samples are based exclusively on auditor's judgment
- Statistical samples involve mathematics and probabilities

Sampling Risk

Audit risk is affected by sampling risk.

- Sample for performance of tests may not be representative of population
- Conclusions drawn may not be same as if sample were representative

Sampling Risk and Tests of Control

When sample not representative in a test of control, two possible errors

Risk of Assessing Risk Too High (Underreliance)—Auditor will conclude that control is not effective when it actually is

- Auditor will inappropriately assess level of control risk at maximum and perform more substantive testing than necessary
- Resulting audit will be inefficient

Risk of Assessing Risk Too Low (Overreliance)—Auditor will conclude that control is effective when it actually is not

- Auditor will inappropriately assess level of control risk below the maximum and perform less substantive testing than necessary
- Resulting audit may be ineffective and auditor may issue inappropriate report

Sampling Risk and Tests of Control (continued)

Sampling errors in tests of controls

TRUE OPERATING EFFECTIVENESS OF THE CONTROLS

The test of controls indicates:	Adequate for planned assessed level of control risk	Inadequate for planned assessed level of control risk
Extent of operating effectiveness is adequate	Correct decision	Incorrect decision (risk of assessing control risk too low)
Extent of operating effectiveness is inadequate	Incorrect decision (risk of assessing control risk too high)	Correct decision

Sampling Risk and Substantive Tests

When sample not representative in a substantive test, two possible errors

1. **Risk of Incorrect Rejection**—Auditor will incorrectly conclude that management assertion is not corroborated

   - Auditor will reject sample
   - Auditor will require inappropriate adjustment or issue inappropriately modified report

2. **Risk of Incorrect Acceptance**—Auditor will incorrectly conclude that management assertion is corroborated

   - Auditor will accept sample
   - Auditor will inappropriately issue unmodified report

Types of Statistical Sampling

There are three types of statistical sampling frequently used in auditing.

1. **Attribute sampling**—generally used for tests of controls

   - Estimate frequency of errors in population based on frequency in sample
   - Determine whether or not estimated error rate indicates control is working effectively

2. **Classical variables sampling**—generally used for substantive testing

   - Estimate value of population based on value of items in sample
   - Determine whether or not estimated value is close enough to management's assertion as to valuation

3. **Probability proportional to size sampling**—also used for substantive testing

   - Form of variables sampling
   - Items that are larger in size or value higher probability of being selected for sample

Attribute Sampling

The auditor determines the control to be tested and identifies the type of error that would indicate the control is not effective so that a sampling plan can be established.

- Establish **tolerable deviation rate**—the maximum error rate the auditor will allow without increasing the assessed level of control risk
- Determine **allowable risk of overreliance** or sampling risk—the maximum allowable risk of assessing control risk too low
- Determine the **expected population deviation rate**—the rate of errors expected to occur in population which is the basis for the initial assessed level of control risk
- Determine the **sample size**
- Select and test the sample

Attribute Sampling (continued)

1) Calculate the sample deviation rate – # of errors in sample ÷ # of items in sample

Determine the **upper deviation limit**—maximum population error rate based on sample deviation rate and acceptable risk of overreliance

Upper precision limit = Sample deviation rate + Allowance for sampling risk

Reach conclusions and document results

- If upper precision limit ≤ tolerable rate—assessed level of control risk unchanged
- If upper precision limit > tolerable rate—assessed level of control risk increased

Calculating Sample Size

Various factors affect sample size

ATTRIBUTES SAMPLING
SUMMARY OF RELATIONSHIPS TO SAMPLE SIZE

Increases in	Effect on Sample Size
Risk of assessing control risk too low (risk of overreliance)	Decrease
Tolerable rate	Decrease
Expected population deviation rate	Increase
Population	Increase (implicit)

Variations of Attribute Sampling

Different approaches can be used when applying attribute sampling.

Under traditional attribute sampling, sample size is determined and sample tested to estimate error rate in population.

Under **stop or go (sequential) sampling,** testing discontinues when auditor acquires sufficient data.

- Appropriate when expected deviation rate is low
- Sample selected in steps
- Each step is based on results of previous step
- No fixed sample size and may result in lower sample if few or no errors detected

Under **discovery sampling**, sample size is very small.

- Appropriate when expected deviation rate is extremely low or zero
- Sample large enough to detect at least one error if it exists
- Any errors in sample result in rejection

Variables Sampling

The auditor determines the balance to be tested and a sampling plan can be established

1) Determine the sample size
   A. Determine allowable risk of incorrect acceptance—the maximum allowable risk that the auditor will accept is an amount that is materially incorrect
   B. Determine the population size
   C. Determine the estimated variability in the population (standard deviation)
   D. Determine the expected amount of misstatement or expected deviation—the amount by which the auditor expects the actual balance to differ from the reported amount based on the assessed level of control risk
   E. Establish tolerable misstatement (allowance for sampling risk)—the maximum difference, taking materiality into account, between the actual balance and the reported balance that will not prevent the auditor from issuing an unmodified report

Variables Sampling (continued)

2) Select and test the sample
3) Evaluate the sample and project to population
   A. Calculate a point estimate (the implied audit value) for the population based on the sample's audited values
   B. Construct a confidence interval to determine whether to accept or reject the client's recorded balance as consistent with the audit evidence
4) Reach conclusions and document results
   - If client's recorded balance falls within the confidence interval—opinion will not require modification
   - If client's recorded balance falls outside the confidence interval—opinion will require modification

Calculating Sample Size

Various factors affect sample size

VARIABLES SAMPLING
SUMMARY OF RELATIONSHIPS TO SAMPLE SIZE

Increases in	Effect on sampling size
Risk—Incorrect Acceptance	Decrease
Risk—Incorrect Rejection	Decrease
Tolerable Misstatement (Error)	Decrease
Expected Misstatement (Error)	Increase
Population	Increase
Variation (Standard Deviation)	Increase

Probability Proportional to Size (PPS) Sampling

PPS, a form of dollar unit sampling, has advantages over classical variables sampling.

- Items with larger dollar amounts have a greater probability of being selected
- An item that is individually material will automatically be selected
- Sample size may be reduced as the same item may be selected more than once
- The sample distribution does not have to be close to the distribution in the population for the sample to be valid
- Sampling can be initiated prior to year-end more easily

Disadvantages of PPS

- Understated items have a lower probability of being selected
- Items with zero or negative balances are not generally included in the sample
- A high frequency of misstatements results in an increase in sample size

PPS is most effective when

- Few or no errors are expected
- The auditor is concerned about overstatement of the account

Probability Proportional to Size (PPS) Sampling (continued)

PPS is applied as follows:

1) Determine the sample size
   A. Determine the reliability factor (from the AICPA table)
      - Determine the desired risk of incorrect acceptance. The higher the risk of incorrect acceptance, the lower the reliability
      - The zero row in the number of overstatements column in the table is used to determine sample size
   B. Determine the tolerable misstatement, net of any expected misstatements
   C. Determine the population book value
2) Calculate the sample interval
3) Select the sample and perform the auditing procedures
4) Calculate the upper limit on misstatement which includes projected error
5) Evaluate sample results and draw conclusion

Selecting the Sample

1) List items in population in logical sequence
2) Add the balances cumulatively
3) Beginning at a random starting point, select every item at the sampling interval. For example, if the sampling interval is 130, select every 130th item

Calculating the Upper Limit on Misstatement

Upper limit on misstatement = Basic precision + Projected misstatement + Incremental allowance

Calculation of the projected misstatement:

1) Determine items in sample containing misstatement
2) If item has dollar amount ≥ sampling interval, misstatement is added to projected misstatement
3) If item has dollar amount < sampling interval, effect of misstatement on projected misstatement must be calculated and added to the projected misstatement
   - Calculate a tainting factor = Amount of misstatement ÷ Dollar amount of item
   - Projected misstatement = Tainting % × Sampling interval

Calculation of basic precision and incremental allowance is beyond the testing requirements in the exam and is not covered here.

AUDITING WITH TECHNOLOGY

Responsibilities in an Information Technology Environment

Audit objectives are the same when financial records are manual or developed in an information technology (IT) environment.

In an IT environment, the auditor should consider

- Client use of computers in significant accounting applications
- Complexity of the entity's computer operations
- Organizational structure of computer processing activities
- Availability of data
- Use of computer assisted audit techniques (CAATS) for audit procedures

Controls in an IT Environment

As a result of limited segregation of duties and a reduced paper audit trail, the auditor will often have to rely more heavily on the ability to reduce control risk rather than detection risk in order to keep audit risk at an acceptably low level.

The objectives of controls in an IT environment are

- Completeness
- Accuracy
- Validity
- Authorization
- Timeliness
- Integrity

Controls will include general controls, application controls, input controls, processing controls, and output controls

Auditing through the Computer

Once the auditor obtains an understanding of internal control, a decision will be made as to the planned assessed level of control risk.

- The auditor may plan to assess control risk at the maximum when the client's computer system is relatively simple and there is a sufficient audit trail.
- When the client's computer system is complex, the lack of an audit trail may prevent the auditor from adequately reducing detection risk through the performance of substantive tests and the auditor will need to set control risk below the maximum. This will require the performance of tests of controls in relation to those control activities on which the auditor intends to rely.

Testing General Control Activities

The auditor will generally first test general control activities. The auditor can test

- Personnel policies by inspecting personnel manuals, observing the appropriate segregation of duties, and verifying restrictions on the access to the system through the use of passwords
- File security by inspecting external labels on files and using the computer to read internal labels, and observing the existence of lockout procedures and file protection
- Contingency plans by observing the existence of multiple generations of backup files, discussing disaster recovery plans with management, and observing the existence of a hot or cold site
- Facilities by observing the appropriateness of the location and the limitations on access and by confirming the existence of insurance
- Access to computer files by verifying the use of passwords to prevent unauthorized individuals from obtaining access

Testing General Control Activities (continued)

In testing controls over the development of, and changes to, programs and systems design, the auditor might

- Make inquiries of personnel
- Review minutes of meetings of computer staff and users
- Inspect documentation of testing performed before programs were put into use
- Review documentation of program changes and compare them to management approvals
- Inspect manuals being used by operators and other users

Testing Application Control Activities

If general controls are in place and operating effectively, reliance may also be placed on application control activities. The auditor can test output controls largely through observation. Input and processing controls, on the other hand, may be tested in a variety of ways.

Computer assisted audit techniques, or **CAATs**, are used to test the operation of software. These include test data, integrated test facilities, tagging and tracing, embedded audit modules, and generalized audit software programs.

Test data include examples of exceptions as well as valid data and are run through the company's computer programs. The auditor compares results to expected results to evaluate the processing of the data and handling of exceptions.

Using an **integrated test facility**, fictitious and real transactions are processed simultaneously using fictitious divisions or departments in the client's system. The auditor can review the client's processing of the data to evaluate the effectiveness of the programs.

Testing Application Control Activities (continued)

By **tagging** transactions, they may be **traced** through the system and the auditor is provided a printout of the steps followed in processing them.

Embedded audit modules are auditor programs inserted into client systems to identify and report certain transactions based on specified criteria.

Generalized audit software packages test the reliability of the client's programs. These packages are used to perform many specific audit procedures. One application is **parallel simulation** in which the software is designed to process data in a manner that is essentially the same as that used by the client's program. The results can then be compared to evaluate the client's processing of the data.

Auditing with the Computer

The auditor may use the computer to perform substantive tests. Once the auditor has access to the client's data, the computer can be used to

- Examine the client's data for validity, completeness, and accuracy
- Rearrange and analyze the client's data
- Select client data for audit samples
- Compare similar data contained in two or more of the client's files to identify discrepancies
- Compare the results of audit procedures, such as test counts, to the client's data

The use of computers in the performance of an audit does not change the auditor's responsibility to adhere to the professional standards. Methods, however, may change. There may be a reduction in the use of working papers, and this will reduce the auditor's ability to observe the details of calculations when reviewing the work of staff assistants.

AUDIT REPORTS

Audit Reports

Be familiar with the key details of the standard reports of

- Auditing Standards Board
- Public Company Accounting Oversight Board

Note: The Auditing Standards Board (and International Auditing Standards) use the term "unmodified" while the PCAOB uses the term "unqualified."

Standard Report

Unmodified Opinion, Nonpublic Company

Required title ("Independent" should be in title)

Addressee (company, board of directors and/or stockholders—**not** management)

Introductory paragraph

1. Identify the entity audited.
2. Financial statements have been audited.
3. Titles of financial statements.
4. Date or period covered by financial statements.

Management's responsibility for the financial statements (section with this heading)

1. Management's responsibility for preparation and fair presentation of the financial statements following applicable financial reporting framework.
2. Responsibility includes design, implementation and maintenance of IC to allow preparation and fair presentation of financial statements that are free of material misstatement from errors or fraud.

Unmodified Opinion, Nonpublic Company (continued)

Auditor's responsibility (section with this heading)

1. Express an opinion based on audit
2. Audit conducted in accordance with Generally Accepted Auditing Standards (GAAS) of USA
3. Standards require auditor to plan and perform audit to obtain reasonable assurance financial statements free of material misstatement.
4. Discuss nature of audit procedures.
5. Audit evidence sufficient and appropriate for opinion.

Opinion (section with this heading)

1. Financial statements present fairly, in all material respects, financial position and results of operations and cash flows in accordance with applicable financial reporting framework.
2. Identify the financial reporting framework.

Manual or printed signature (firm name)

Auditor's address (city and state)

Date (no earlier than date auditor has obtained sufficient appropriate audit evidence)

Unqualified Opinion, Public Company (PCAOB)

Required title ("Report of Independent Registered Public Accounting Firm")

Addressee (stockholders and board of directors)

Opinion on the Financial Statements (with this heading)

1. Identify entity audited
2. Financial statements have been audited
3. Titles of financial statements
4. Date or period covered by financial statements
5. Financial statements present fairly, in all material respects, financial position and results of operations and cash flows in accordance with applicable financial reporting framework
6. Identify financial reporting framework

Unqualified Opinion, Public Company (PCAOB) (continued)

Basis for Opinion (with this heading)

1. Financial statements are management's responsibility
2. Expressing opinion is auditor's responsibility
3. Audit conducted in accordance with PCAOB standards
4. Standards require auditor to plan and perform audit to obtain reasonable assurance financial statements free of material misstatement
5. Discuss nature of audit procedures (less detailed than AICPA)
6. Audit provides reasonable basis for opinion
7. Auditor independent and registered with PCAOB

Unqualified Opinion, Public Company (PCAOB) (continued)

Critical Audit Matters (with this heading)

1. Significant audit areas in which challenging, subjective, or complex auditor judgments were made
2. For each critical audit matter:
   a. How identified
   b. How addressed
   c. Refer to related financial statement accounts or disclosures

Manual or printed signature (firm name)

Identify year auditor began serving consecutively as company auditor

Auditor's address (city, state)

Date (no earlier than date auditor has obtained sufficient appropriate audit evidence)

Note: If the report on internal control over financial reporting is issued separately, an additional paragraph is added immediately after the opinion paragraph, referring to the internal control report.

Group Financial Statement Audit Reports

This situation arises when more than one audit firm is involved in the audit of a particular year.

- Example: Your firm audited the entire company except for one subsidiary.

A group engagement partner and team are determined based on which firm has performed most of the work and has the greatest knowledge of the overall financial statements. The group engagement partner is responsible for the audit and report.

The group engagement team should obtain an understanding of:

- Whether the component auditor is competent and understands and will comply with all ethical requirements, particularly independence
- The extent to which the group engagement team will be involved with the component auditor
- Whether the group engagement team will be able to obtain necessary information on the consolidation process from the component auditor
- Whether the component auditor operates in a regulatory environment that actively oversees auditors

(Additional audit procedures by the group engagement team depend upon information obtained relating to the above bullets.)

Group Financial Statement Audit Reports (continued)

The group engagement partner decides whether to take responsibility for work of component (other) auditor

- If responsibility taken, the other auditor is not mentioned in the audit report
- If responsibility not taken, the other auditor is mentioned in the audit report

When a group auditor is not satisfied with the work of the component auditor, the group auditor should either

- Reperform the work or
- Treat it as a scope limitation and modify the audit report opinion

Division of Responsibility

Group Auditor Does Not Take Responsibility

A division of responsibility must be clearly indicated in report.

Modifications to the report

- Will be specific as to the portions of the work performed by the component auditor
- Will not generally name component auditor, although component auditor may be named if permission is received and component auditor report is included in the document containing the financial statements

Group Auditor Takes Responsibility

Standard unmodified report may be issued, but group engagement team should perform additional procedures as indicated in the next focus note:

Auditing of Components

Component Nature	Audit Procedures
Not significant	The group engagement team should perform analytical procedures at the group level. Audit additional components *if* sufficient appropriate audit evidence has not been obtained.
Significant due to its individual financial significance to the group.	1. The group auditor or component auditor should perform audit of component, adapted as necessary to the needs of the group engagement team, using the materiality of the component. 2. The group engagement team should be involved in the risk assessment and should: • Discuss with the component auditor or the component management the component's business activities of significance to the group. • Discuss with the component auditor the susceptibility of the component to material misstatement. • Review the component auditor's documentation of identified significant risks of material misstatement of the group financial statements.

Auditing of Components (continued)

Component Nature	Audit Procedures

Significant because it is likely to include significant risks of material misstatement of the group financial statements.	1. The group auditor or the component auditor should perform one or more of:
	  • Audit component, adapted as necessary to the needs of the group engagement team, using the materiality of the component.
	  • Audit one or more component account balances, classes of transactions or disclosures that relate to the significant risks.
	  • Perform specified audit procedures relating to the likely significant risks of material misstatement of the group financial statements.
	2. Requirement 2 on the previous page.

Unmodified Opinion with Emphasis-of-Matter Paragraphs

Sometimes required by professional standards, sometimes at the discretion (choice) of the auditor

Treatment

- Include it *after* the opinion paragraph for nonpublic companies.
    - Public companies: Although not specifically required for all, most appear after opinion paragraph; consistency and going concern should be after the opinion paragraph.
- Use the heading "Emphasis-of-matter" or other appropriate heading for nonpublic and public companies.
- Include in the paragraph a clear reference to the matter emphasized and where that matter is in the financial statements.
- Indicate that the auditor's opinion is not modified with respect to the matter emphasized.

Circumstances

- Substantial doubt about ability to continue as a going concern
- Inconsistency in application of accounting principles
- Uncertainties
- Other circumstances at discretion of auditor

Substantial Doubt about Ability to Continue as a Going Concern

An audit considers whether there is substantial doubt about an entity's ability to continue as a going concern for a reasonable period.

- A reasonable period may be up to one year after the date that the financial statements are issued or available to be issued

Management may be required to provide a going concern evaluation, e.g., required by FASB and GASB

- If provided, the auditor assesses management's evaluation
- If not provided, the auditor discusses with management whether going concern problems exist

Conditions such as the following may raise going concern doubts

- Operating losses, negative cash flows, or other negative trends
- Loan defaults, dividend arrearages, or other indications of financial difficulty
- Labor difficulties or other internal matters
- Obsolescence of patents, declining industry, or other external matters

Substantial Doubt about Ability to Continue as a Going Concern (continued)

Although an audit does not include audit procedures aimed directly at addressing going concern, the following procedures may reveal going concern doubts:

- Analytical procedures
- Review of subsequent events
- Examination of debt agreements to determine compliance
- Reading of minutes of board meetings
- Making inquiry of legal counsel
- Confirming with others arrangements for financial support

Substantial Doubt about Ability to Continue as a Going Concern (continued)

When there may be substantial doubt about going concern status, auditors consider management's plans to address that doubt, such as by:

- Disposing of assets
- Borrowing money or restructuring debt
- Reducing or delaying expenditures
- Increasing ownership equity

Note: The auditor is required to evaluate whether it is probable that management's plans can be implemented and would effectively mitigate the going concern problems.

Audit reports

- If doubt no longer remains, issue a standard unmodified report
- If doubt remains, issue an unmodified report with an emphasis-of-matter paragraph following the opinion paragraph

Substantial Doubt about Ability to Continue as a Going Concern (continued)

- If, in any situation, management does not include needed disclosures related to the matter, a departure from GAAP exists, which will lead to a qualified or adverse opinion
- If the use of going concern basis is considered inappropriate, issue an adverse opinion

Inconsistency in Application of GAAP

Changes in accounting principles that result in a consistency modification

- A change from one acceptable principle to another
- A change from an unacceptable principle to an acceptable one
- A change in principle that is inseparable from a change in estimate
- A change in the method of accounting for investments
- A change in the companies included in consolidated financial statements
- A correction of an error

Changes in accounting principles that do not result in a consistency modification

- A change in accounting estimate
- A change in classification
- Adoption of a principle for a new transaction

Inconsistency in Application of GAAP (continued)

When auditor determines that the inconsistency is justified

- Unmodified opinion expressed
- Emphasis-of-matter paragraph added after the opinion paragraph to emphasize the inconsistency

When auditor determines that the inconsistency is not justified

- Qualified or adverse opinion expressed (this is a departure from GAAP)

Uncertainties

1) Proper accounting for an uncertainty:

Likelihood of loss	Amount of loss estimable	Amount of loss not estimable
Probable	Accrue and disclose	Disclose only
Reasonably possible	Disclose only	Disclose only
Remote	Neither accrue nor disclose	Neither accrue nor disclose

2) When the uncertainty is properly presented, auditor reporting choices:
- Standard unmodified.
- Unmodified opinion with an emphasis-of-matter paragraph added following opinion paragraph.

Uncertainties (continued)

- Disclaimer of opinion for multiple uncertainties with a basis for modification paragraph (prior to opinion paragraph).

- Note that whether to include an emphasis-of-matter paragraph is entirely up to the auditor (*at auditor's discretion*) as it is not required by the standards—unlike the situation for the previous two areas, substantial doubt about going concern and inconsistency.

3) When management does not properly account for the uncertainty, a qualified or adverse opinion is appropriate (this is a departure from GAAP)

Other Circumstances at Discretion of Auditor

1) An auditor may, on a discretionary basis, emphasize a matter relating to the financial statements.
2) Auditor believes users will better understand information in financial statements or report with additional information.
3) Auditor adds emphasis-of-matter paragraph following the opinion paragraph.

Items that might be emphasized in an explanatory paragraph may include

- A major catastrophe that affects the entity's financial position
- Significant transactions with related parties
- Unusually important subsequent events

Note: The matter emphasized is included in the financial statements (emphasizing a matter concerning the scope of the audit is not appropriate).

Unmodified Opinions with Other-Matter Paragraphs

Situations presented

- Comparative financial statements
- Other information in documents containing audited financial statements
- Required supplementary information
- Supplementary information in relation to the financial statements as a whole
- Alerts as to report intended use (restricting the use of an auditor's report)
- Additional circumstances

Comparative Financial Statements

When financial statements for two or more periods are presented in comparative form, the auditor's report applies to all of the financial statements presented.

Prior Period Financial Statements Not Audited (That Is, They Are Reviewed, Compiled, or There Is No CPA Association)

- An emphasis-of-matter paragraph is added indicating the nature of CPA association with the prior period financial statements (or indicating that there is no association).

Opinion on Prior Period Statements Different from Opinion Previously Issued

- Other-matter paragraph added and includes the date of the previous report, the type of opinion previously issued, the reasons for the different opinion, and that the opinion is amended.

Comparative Financial Statements (continued)

Prior Period Financial Statements Audited by a Predecessor Auditor

The successor auditor has a choice as to whether to ask the predecessor to reissue the audit report on the preceding period(s).

- If the predecessor's audit report is reissued, the financial statements will have two audit reports—one on year 1 (predecessor's report) and one on year 2 (successor's report).
- If the predecessor auditor's report is not reissued, an other-matter paragraph is added to the successor auditor's report indicating
  - Financial statements of the prior period were audited by a predecessor auditor.
  - Type of opinion expressed by the predecessor and, if the opinion was modified, the reasons therefor.
  - Nature of an emphasis-of-matter paragraph or other-matter paragraph included in the predecessor auditor's report, if any.
  - Date of that report.

Other Information Included with the Audited Financial Statements

This is financial and nonfinancial information (other than required supplementary information) that is included in a document (e.g., an annual report) that has audited financial statements

- Required procedure: Auditors read information for inconsistencies, if any, with the financial statements
- Reporting when no inconsistencies identified—No modification of the audit report
- Reporting when inconsistencies are identified
    - If financial statements are incorrect—This is a departure from GAAP, qualified or adverse opinion
    - If other information is incorrect, request revision—If management refuses, add an other-matter paragraph, withhold audit report, or withdraw from the engagement; opinion remains unmodified

Required Supplementary Information

Required supplementary information is not part of audited financial statements

- Auditor responsible for applying limited procedures, e.g.:
    - Inquire of management how information was prepared
    - Compare information for consistency with financials
    - Obtain written representations of management responsibility
- Auditor reporting when supplemental information is properly presented
    - Nonpublic company—Add other-matter paragraph indicating that while limited procedures have been performed on the information, no opinion is expressed
    - Public company—No report modification is necessary
- Auditor reporting when supplemental information is not properly presented
    - Other-matter paragraph (or explanatory paragraph for PCAOB) added, but opinion paragraph not modified

Supplementary Information in Relation to the Financial Statements as a Whole

This may apply to either of the preceding two sections on other or required supplementary information or to other supplementary information.

- Here the client desires a report on whether the supplementary information is fairly stated, in all material respects, in relation to the financial statements as a whole
- The CPA must have audited the financial statements
- Procedures applied to the supplementary information include inquiries and various general procedures
- If the information is fairly presented in relation to the financial statements, the CPA issues a report so indicating

Alerts as to Intended Use

Certain circumstances will make it appropriate to restrict distribution or use of an auditor's report.

- When financial statements are prepared according to provisions of **contractual agreements,** the report should be restricted to parties to the contract
- When financial statements are prepared according to **regulations,** the report should be restricted to the regulatory agency
- When the report indicates the findings of **agreed-upon procedures**, the report should be restricted to the parties agreeing upon the procedures

The client should be informed of the restriction

The report should include a final paragraph stating the restriction

Additional Circumstances Involving Other-Matter Paragraphs

Circumstance	Content of Other-Matter Paragraph
Comparative statements (assume two years being presented, with first year not audited).	State that the prior period financial statements are unaudited.
Special purpose financial statements prepared in accordance with a *contractual* or *regulatory* basis of accounting.	Restrict use of audit report to those within entity, parties to the contractor agreement, or the regulatory agencies to whose jurisdiction the entity is subject. (In the case of regulatory basis financial statement, issuance of a general use audit report is also possible.)
In rare circumstances an auditor may legally be unable to withdraw from an engagement even when a pervasive limitation of the scope of the audit has been imposed by management.	Explain why it is not possible for the auditor to withdraw (also disclaim an opinion).
An entity prepares sets of financial statements in accordance with more than one general purpose framework (for example, one set of financial statements following GAAP and another following IFRS)	The auditor may issue reports on each and refer to the fact that another set of financial statements has been prepared using the other general purpose framework and the auditor also has reported on those financial statements.

Modified Opinions—Two Circumstances

1. Materially misstated financial statements (departures from GAAP)
2. Inability to obtain sufficient appropriate audit evidence (scope limitations)

Materially Misstated Financial Statements (Departures from GAAP)

Examples of departures from GAAP include

- Principles not generally accepted
- Principles are not appropriate under the circumstances
- Information in the financial statements is not classified and summarized in reasonable manner
- Financial statements do not fairly present financial position, results of operations, and cash flows within a range of acceptable limits
- Required disclosures are missing or erroneously presented

Materially Misstated Financial Statements (Departures from GAAP) (continued)

Materiality

The materiality of a departure from GAAP will determine its effect on the auditor's report.

- If not material, unmodified report
- If material, qualified opinion
- If material and pervasive, adverse opinion

Pervasive—One or more of

- Not confined to specific elements, accounts, or items of financial statements
- If confined, a substantial proportion of financial statements
- Disclosures fundamental to users' understanding of financial statements

Details of Report Modification

Effects on auditor's report (whether qualified or adverse) in two ways

1. Basis for modification paragraph added before opinion paragraph
2. Opinion paragraph refers to departure from GAAP and is either qualified or adverse.

> *Qualified: "In our opinion, except for the effects of..., the financial statements referred to above..."*

> *Adverse: "In our opinion, because of the effects of the matters discussed in the preceding paragraph, the financial statements referred to above do not present fairly..."*

Inability to Obtain Sufficient Appropriate Audit Evidence (Scope Limitations)

Types of Scope Limitations

Scope limitations are restrictions on the actions of the auditor.

- Prevent auditor from performing procedures as planned
- May result from three circumstances

    1. Circumstances beyond client control (e.g., records destroyed by fire)
    2. Circumstances relating to timing of auditor's work (e.g., hired too late to observe inventory)
    3. Client (e.g., refuses to allow auditor to confirm receivable)

Inability to Obtain Sufficient Appropriate Audit Evidence (continued)

Overcoming Scope Limitations

Auditor may be able to overcome scope limitations

- Assertion that cannot be corroborated may not be material to financial statements taken as a whole
- Auditor may be able to apply alternate procedures

When auditor can overcome scope limitation, a standard unmodified report may be issued

When auditor is not able to overcome the scope limitation, if the possible effect on the financial statements is:

- Immaterial—Unmodified opinion
- Material, not pervasive—Qualified opinion
- Material and pervasive—Disclaimer of opinion

Details of Report Modification

Details on effects on auditor's report

- Basis for modification paragraph indicating reasons for inability to obtain sufficient appropriate audit evidence added preceding the opinion paragraph
- Heading of opinion paragraph titled "Qualified Opinion" (or "Disclaimer of Opinion")
- Opinion paragraph modified

    Qualified Opinion: Indicate that except for the possible effects of the matter described in the basis for qualified opinion paragraph the financial statements follow GAAP.

    Disclaimer of Opinion: Indicate because of possible effects unable to obtain sufficient appropriate audit evidence and do not express an opinion.

- Auditor responsibility paragraph

    Qualified Opinion: State audit evidence sufficient and appropriate to issue modified audit opinion.

    Disclaimer of Opinion: Modified to indicate auditor unable to obtain sufficient appropriate audit evidence to provide a basis for an opinion.

Financial Statements Prepared Using Another Country's Framework

Example: A US-based company prepares financial statements for a foreign subsidiary for use in that foreign country

When financial statements intended only for use outside the US, auditor may

- Issue a US form report indicating financial statements prepared in accordance with financial reporting framework generally accepted in another country, or
- Issue other country audit report

When financial statements intended both for use outside and inside US, a second report is also issued:

- Emphasis-of-matter paragraph added saying basis differs from GAAP; an unmodified opinion may be issued.

Summary Financial Statements

Auditor may report on summary (condensed) financial statements

Report should indicate

- That the complete financial statements were audited and that an opinion was expressed
- The date of the auditor's report on the complete financial statements
- The type of opinion expressed
- Whether the information is fairly stated in all material respects in relation to the complete financial statements

Reviews of Quarterly (Interim) Information

Objective—provide accountant with a basis for communicating whether s/he is aware of any material modifications that should be made to the interim financial information to conform with applicable financial reporting framework.

May only be performed by the auditor of last year's financial statements or the auditor engaged to audit this year's financial statements.

Composed of inquiries and analytical procedures. Also, the auditor, for only this type of review, is required to have an understanding of internal control.

The report includes limited (negative) assurance

OTHER TYPES OF REPORTS

Reports on Application of Framework Requirements

Situation is that a CPA is asked to report on proposed accounting for a transaction.

CPA should make certain that s/he understands details of the transaction.

Such a report should not be issued on a hypothetical transaction that does not involve facts or circumstances relating to the specific company.

Financial Statements with Special Purpose Frameworks

Illustrations: cash basis, tax basis, regulatory basis, contractual basis.

Do not use the terms *balance sheet*, *income statement*, etc.

The following table summarizes important information relating to special purpose financial reporting frameworks.

Financial Statements with Special Purpose Frameworks (continued)

	Cash Basis or Tax Basis	Contractual Basis	Regulatory Basis	Regulatory Basis (General Use Statements)	Other Basis
Opinion(s)	Single opinion on special purpose framework	Single opinion on special purpose framework	Single opinion on special purpose framework	Dual opinion on special purpose framework and on GAAP	Single opinion on special purpose framework
Description of purpose for which special purpose financial statements are prepared	No	Yes	Yes	Yes	If alert required by AU-C 905
Alert in an emphasis-of-matter paragraph alerting users that the special purpose framework is other than GAAP	Yes	Yes	Yes	No	No
Alert in an other-matter paragraph as to intended use of auditor's report	No	Yes	Yes	No	If required by AU-C 905
Additional requirements unique to category.		The auditors should obtain an understanding of significant management interpretations of the contract.	If a specific layout, form or wording is required that the auditor has no basis to make, the auditor should reword the form or attach an appropriately worded separate report.		

Audits of Single Financial Statements and Specific Elements, Accounts, or Items

Such engagements may be performed.

The audit report is on the single financial statement or elements, account, or item.

If element involves stockholders' equity, auditor performs procedures sufficient to enable opinion on financial position.

If element involves net income, auditor performs procedures sufficient to enable opinion on financial position and results of operations.

Reporting on Compliance

Compliance with Aspects of Contractual Agreements or Regulatory Requirements in Connection with Audited Financial Statements

The auditor's report on compliance

- States that the financial statements were audited
- Refers to the specific covenant or paragraphs of the agreement and provides negative assurance relative to compliance (i.e., "nothing came to our attention that caused us to believe that XYZ Company failed to comply with the terms of…")
- Describes any significant interpretations made by management relating to the agreement, if any

When the auditor has identified one or more items of noncompliance, those items are identified in the report.

Service Organization Control (SOC) Reports

Types of reports

- SOC 1: Restricted use reports on controls at a service organization relevant to a user entity's internal control over financial reporting
- SOC 2: Restricted use reports on controls at a service organization related to security, availability, processing integrity, confidentiality, and/or privacy
- SOC 3: General use SysTrust reports related to security, availability, processing integrity, confidentiality, and/or privacy

Reports on Processing of Transactions by Service Organizations (SOC 1 Report)

Two Types of SOC 1 Reports

Type 1 reports: Reasonable assurance as of a *specific date* that

1) Management's description of service organization's system is fairly represented
2) Controls are suitably designed to achieve control objectives

Type 2 reports: Reasonable assurance for a *specified time period* that

1) Management's description of service organization's system is fairly represented,
2) Controls are suitably designed to achieve control objectives, and
3) Controls operated effectively.

Letters to Underwriters

Accountants provide letters to underwriters (comfort letters) in connection with the registration of securities with the SEC

- Dated same date or just before registration statement becomes effective
- Accountant's involvement limited to negative assurance
- Not required under Securities Act of 1933 and copies not filed with SEC

Subjects covered in a comfort letter may include

- Independence of accountants
- Whether audited financial statements and schedules comply in all material respects with requirements of Securities Act of 1933
- Unaudited financial statements, condensed interim information, pro forma financial statements, financial forecasts, and changes in items prepared or occurring after the date of the latest financial statements included in the registration statement
- Tables, statistics, and other information included in the registration statement
- Negative assurance as to compliance of nonfinancial information in registration statement to requirements of Regulation S-K

Governmental Auditing and Compliance Audits

Governmental audits refer to audits of

- Governmental entities
- Entities receiving governmental financial assistance

Audit is conducted under one or more of

- Generally Accepted Auditing Standards (GAAS)
- Government Auditing Standards (GAGAS)
- The Single Audit Act (SAA)

Government Auditing Standards (GAGAS)

Audits under GAGAS provide reasonable assurance of detecting material misstatements that

- Result from noncompliance with contract provisions or grant agreements
- Have a direct and material effect on the financial statements

GAGAS standards for fieldwork and reporting exceed standards under GAAS

The auditor's **written reports** under GAGAS include

- An opinion on the financial statements
- Information regarding the consideration of internal control
- Information regarding the compliance with laws and regulations

Government Auditing Standards (GAGAS) (continued)

As to the consideration of **internal control,** the report will indicate

- The scope of testing of controls
- Whether opinion on IC provided
- Identified deficiencies in internal control

As to **compliance** with laws and regulations, the report will indicate

- The scope of compliance testing
- Whether opinion on compliance provided
- Any material instances of fraud and illegal acts discovered

Single Audit Act (SAA)

SAA applies to state and local governments, institutions of higher education, and other nonprofit organizations receiving federal financial assistance (FFA)

- Must engage auditor to perform single coordinated audit if federal grant expenditures equal to or greater than $750,000
- Audit relates to requirements of applicable FFA program

The report covers the financial statements, compliance with laws and regulations, and internal controls

In addition, the auditor reports on

- Compliance with general requirements applying to FFA programs
- Compliance with specific requirements of major federal programs
- Compliance with specific requirements of nonmajor federal programs tested

Focus on

Other Types of Reports

224

Major Federal Programs

Major federal programs are identified on the basis of

- Expenditures exceeding certain amounts in relation to total expenditures of all FFA received during the year
- An analysis of risk assessment

Materiality is determined in relation to each program

Management identifies federal programs providing funding including

- Funds received directly from federal agencies
- Funds received indirectly from federal agencies through state and local government agencies or nonprofit organizations

Auditor Responsibility

An auditor under the SAA must apply GAAS and GAGAS

When assessing risk, the auditor includes the risk of failure to modify the report despite noncompliance with the requirements of a specific program

- Inherent risk is modified to include the risk that material noncompliance could occur if there were no related controls
- Control risk is modified to include the risk that noncompliance may not be prevented or detected by the entity's controls
- Detection risk is modified to include the risk that audit procedures will not detect material noncompliance

The auditor reports on whether the entity has controls to provide reasonable assurance of compliance. The auditor

- Evaluates the effectiveness of controls designed to detect noncompliance
- Determines if there are controls to ensure compliance
- Documents procedures used to assess and test internal control

Focus on

Other Types of Reports

226

Testing for Compliance

When testing for compliance with requirements of major FFA programs, the auditor must consider

- Activities that may or not be funded under a program
- Cost accounting principles that must be applied
- Procedures to minimize the time between receiving and spending of funds
- Criteria related to eligibility for the programs
- Standards for the use and disposition of assets acquired with federal funds
- Requirements for contributions of resources by the recipient of federal funds
- Incurring of funded costs during the funding period
- Restrictions on contracting with parties disqualified from participation
- Recording and use of income generated from a federal program
- Reporting using standard forms
- Monitoring activities of subrecipients
- Special provisions of each federal program

Reports under the SAA

Upon completion of an audit under the SAA, the auditor will issue a report that complies with requirements of GAAS and GAGAS as well as reports that are specific to the entity's federal awards.

Reporting requirements under the SAA include

- Conformity with GAAP
- Fair presentation of the schedule of expenditures of federal awards
- Internal control as related to the financial statements and to major programs
- Compliance with laws, regulations, and provisions of contracts or grant agreements
- The schedule of federal awards listing total expenditures for each award
- Reportable conditions (material weaknesses and significant deficiencies) related to internal control over major programs
- Material noncompliance with laws, regulations, and contract or grant provisions
- Questioned costs in excess of $25,000
- Known fraud affecting a federal award

Summary of Relationship among GAAS, GAGAS, and SAA

Procedures Required	GAAS	GAGAS	SAA
Audit of financial statements in accordance with specific standards	✓	✓	✓
Compliance with laws and regulations	✓	✓	✓
Internal controls	✓	✓	✓
Compliance with general requirements			✓
Compliance with specific requirements applicable to FFA programs			✓
Understanding of specific internal controls relevant to FFA			✓

Summary of Relationship among GAAS, GAGAS, and SAA (continued)

Reports Issued	GAAS	GAGAS	SAA
Opinion on financial statements	✓	✓	✓
Written report on compliance with laws and regulations		✓	✓
Written report on internal controls		✓	✓
Report on a list of total expenditures for each federal award			✓
Prepare a schedule of reportable conditions, material noncompliance, questioned costs, and known fraud			✓

ACCOUNTING AND REVIEW SERVICES

- The AICPA's Accounting and Review Services Committee promulgates (issues) standards for these services
- Types of accounting and review services include financial statement

  - Preparation
  - Compilation
  - Review

Financial Statement Preparation

- Accountant prepares financial statements using the records, documents, explanations, and other information provided by management; required:
    - Identification of applicable financial reporting framework (e.g., GAAP)
    - Preparation following framework
    - Inclusion of adequate description of framework

- Examples of services covered by the standard include preparation of
    - Financial statements prior to audit or review by *another* accountant
    - Financial statements to be presented alongside the entity's tax return
    - Personal financial statements for inclusion alongside a financial plan
    - A single financial statement
    - Financial statements with disclosures omitted

Financial Statement Preparation (continued)

- Examples of services **not** covered by the standard include
  - Assisting with adjusting entries or maintaining certain schedules (e.g., depreciation)
  - Entering general ledger transactions or processing payments in an accounting software system
  - Drafting financial statement notes
  - Preparing financial statements in conjunction with
    - Litigation services
    - Business valuation services
    - Solely for inclusion with a tax return

Overall Requirements

- Establish understanding with management or those charged with governance and document it through an engagement letter or similar form of written documentation.
- Discuss with management important judgments made during engagement
- Understand the financial reporting framework
- Disclose departures from financial reporting framework in the financial statements (if management will not correct)
- Accountant need not determine whether he or she is independent
- Generally no accountant's report issued if financial statements indicate "no assurance is provided" on each page
    - If not so disclosed, a report with disclaimer is added

Compilations

- A compilation involves assisting management in presenting financial information in the form of financial statements
- Accountant must have knowledge of accounting principles followed
- At a minimum accountant must read the compiled statements for appropriate format and obvious misstatements
    - If misstated and client will not correct, accountant should withdraw
- Beyond the above, accountant has no responsibility to perform investigative procedures
- A disclaimer of opinion is issued

Planning

Establish and document understanding with management (or those charged with governance) and document in an engagement letter or other suitable form of written agreement.

- If unfamiliar with client business, can accept if competent before compilation
- Independence not required
- May use financial reporting framework other than GAAP if that basis is properly disclosed.

Compilation Report

Report on compilation of financial statements of nonpublic company should state

- Compilation performed in accordance with SSARS issued by the AICPA
- Management responsible for financial statements prepared in accordance with GAAP.
- Compilation limited to presenting management's information in the form of financial statements
- Financial statements not audited or reviewed
- Accountant does not express opinion or provide any other form of assurance

In addition

- City and state of accountant's office
- Report dated as of completion of compilation
- Each page of compiled financial statements may, but is not required to, refer to report

    "See Accountant's Compilation Report"

An accountant need not be independent to perform a compilation.

When not independent, last paragraph of report should so indicate

    "We are not independent with respect to X Company"

Other Considerations

Compilations—Omission of Disclosures

Accountant may compile financial statements of nonpublic company when substantially all disclosures omitted

- Omission must be indicated in report which should indicate that the financial statements are not designed for those who are not informed about such matters
- Omission not intended to make financial statements misleading

Compilations—Supplementary Information Accompanies Financial Statements

- Indicate degree of responsibility (if any) being taken for that information either in compilation report (add other matter paragraph) or as a separate report

Reviews

The objective of a review is to provide objective limited (negative) assurance that no material modifications to financials needed

- A review is an assurance and attest engagement
- Planning reviews
    - Obtain engagement letter or other suitable form of written communication signed by accountant and management, or those charged with governance.
    - Obtain an understanding of the industry and knowledge of the client
    - Procedures required
        - Analytical procedures
        - Inquiries of management
        - Written representations from management
        - If "unexpected results" are found: make inquiries to management

Reviews (continued)

- Other procedures
  - Minutes of stockholder and director meetings
  - Interim financial information
  - Obtain reports from other accountants who have reviewed significant components of the company
- A review does *not* contemplate
  - Internal control
  - Assessing fraud risk
  - Tests of accounting records
  - Examination of source documents

Reviews (continued)

- Should have representation letter signed by management acknowledging responsibility for
    - Fair presentation of the financial statements
    - Complete and truthful responses to all inquiries
    - Prevention and detection of fraud and disclosure to CPA of suspected fraud
- May use financial reporting framework other than GAAP if that basis is properly disclosed.
- An accountant must be independent to perform a review

Performing Analytical Procedures

The CPA must form expectations about the numbers in financial statements being reviewed

- Expectations are predictions of what the recorded amounts and ratios will be.
- These are developed by identifying plausible relationships based on the CPA's knowledge of the client and industry.
- Sources of expectations include prior periods, budgets, industry data, and nonfinancial data.
- The CPA must document significant expectations and identify the factors considered in developing them.

Performing Analytical Procedures (continued)

Examples of inquiries and analytical procedures performed in a review include

- Inquire about accounting principles
- Inquire about procedures for recording, classifying, and summarizing information for financial statements
- Identify unusual relationships and unusual items using analytical procedures
- Inquire about actions taken at meetings of shareholders, directors, or others that may affect financial statements
- Read financial statements to determine if they appear to conform with GAAP
- Obtain reports from other accountants auditing or reviewing components of the financial statements
- Inquire of individuals responsible for financial and accounting matters
- Accountant does not obtain understanding of internal control or assess control risk
    - Note that this is different from a review of interim financial statements which requires an understanding of internal control

Review Report

A review report should be issued that includes

- Title with word "independent"
- Appropriate addressee—ordinarily those for whom report is prepared (examples: company itself, those charged with governance, partners, proprietor)
- Introductory paragraph with
  - Name of entity reviewed
  - Identification of financial statements (and their date) and statement that financial statements were reviewed
  - Review includes primarily analytical procedures and inquiries of management
  - Review substantially less in scope than an audit
  - No opinion expressed
- "Management Responsibility" and "Accountant Responsibility" sections
- Concluding section about whether accountant is aware of any material modifications needed
- Manual or printed firm signature, city and state accountant practices in, and date of report (no earlier than date accountant has completed procedures sufficient to obtain limited assurance)

Departures from GAAP

Accountant may become aware of material departure from GAAP

- • Should request that financial statements be revised
- • If not revised, should consider modification of report
- • If modification not adequate, accountant should consider withdrawing from engagement

Additional Review Issues

- Going Concern—Consider whether anything comes to accountant's attention indicating uncertainty as to ability to continue as a going concern
  - Financial statements should indicate such uncertainty; if they do not, treat as departure from GAAP
- Subsequent Events
  - Financial statements should disclose events; if they do not, treat as departure from GAAP
- Subsequent Discovery of Facts After Report Release
  - Treat as in audits (management should revise financial statements if so needed)
    - If management refuses to revise, ultimately, take action to prevent use of the review report.
- Reference to Work of Other Accountants Involved with Significant Components—treat as audit (refer to if accountant does not wish to take responsibility for work of other accountants)

Other Compilation and Review Considerations

Fraud and Illegal Acts in Compilation or Review Engagements

The CPA has certain responsibilities regarding fraud and illegal acts in a compilation or review

- Establishing an understanding with the client before commencement of the engagement that the CPA will inform the appropriate level of management of any evidence that fraud or an illegal act may have occurred
- Reporting such evidence when it comes to the CPA's attention unless the matter is clearly inconsequential
- In a review, performing additional procedures as necessary to establish that no material modifications need to made to the financial statements as a result of the suspected fraud or illegal act
- Documenting any communications with management regarding fraud and illegal acts

Restricted Use Compilation and Review Reports

The CPA may issue reports that are restricted to use by specific parties.

- Required when presentation is based on criteria in contractual agreements or regulatory provisions not in conformity with GAAP or other comprehensive basis of accounting
- A separate paragraph must be added to the report indicating
  - That the report is intended solely for specified parties
  - The identity of those specified parties
  - That the report is not intended for anyone other than the specified parties

A CPA may compile specified elements, accounts, or items of a financial statement.

- The CPA who prepares or assists a client in preparing a schedule of such elements may be associated with the schedule and need to issue a report to avoid inappropriate assumptions by a potential user of the level of assurance.
- Normal compilation standards apply including the possibility of restricted use.

A CPA may report on compiled pro forma financial information based on historical statements.

Downgrading Engagements

Accountant may be asked to downgrade an engagement that has begun.

- Audit may be downgraded to review or compilation
- Review may be downgraded to compilation

Before accepting downgrade, accountant should consider

- Reason given by client
- Additional effort to complete original engagement
- Additional cost to complete original engagement

Comparative Financial Statements

Overall guidance when portions of comparative financial statements are not audited

- An entity may include financial information with which the accountant is not associated (e.g., statement audited last year by a different auditor) in a report that also includes information with which the accountant is associated (e.g., this year's compilation)
  - The accountant should not allow his/her name to be associated with the portion of financial statements s/he is not associated with

- A continuing accountant who performs the same or a **higher level of service** this year (e.g., review) than last year (e.g., compilation) should update his/her report on the financial statements of a prior period presented with those of the current period

- A continuing accountant who performs a **lower level of service** should either
  - Include a separate paragraph in his/her report with a description of the responsibility assumed for the prior period statements, or
  - Reissue his/her report on the financial statements of the prior period.

OTHER PROFESSIONAL SERVICES

Reporting on Internal Control in an Integrated Audit

The audit of internal control over financial reporting should be integrated with the audit of the financial statements

- Objective
    - To express an opinion on the effectiveness of the company's internal control over financial reporting
        - Must plan and perform the audit to obtain **competent evidence** that is **sufficient** to obtain **reasonable assurance** about whether **material weaknesses** exist
- **Planning** the audit should include evaluating
    - Matters affecting company industry or business organization
    - The auditor's preliminary judgments about materiality and risk
    - Control deficiencies previously communicated to the audit committee or management

Reporting on Internal Control in an Integrated Audit (continued)

- Legal or regulatory matters
- The type and extent of available evidence related to the effectiveness of the company's internal control over financial reporting
- Public information about the company
- Likelihood of material financial statement misstatements
- Effectiveness of the company's internal control over financial reporting
- Knowledge about risks related to the company evaluated as part of the auditor's client acceptance and retention evaluation

- Role of risk assessment
  - Determine significant accounts and disclosures
  - Select controls to test
  - Determine evidence necessary for a given control
  - Scale the audit by the complexity of the company

Reporting on Internal Control in an Integrated Audit (continued)

- Addressing the risk of fraud: assessing controls over
  - Significant, unusual transactions or unusual journal entries
  - Related-party transactions
  - Significant management estimates
  - Incentives for management to falsify or inappropriately manage financial results
- Using the work of others: the auditor should assess
  - The competence of the persons used
    - Evaluate factors about the person's qualifications and ability to perform the work the auditor plans to use

Reporting on Internal Control in an Integrated Audit (continued)

- The objectivity of the persons used
  - Evaluate whether factors are present that either inhibit or promote a person's ability to perform
- Personnel such as internal auditors normally are expected to have greater competence and objectivity
- As risk associated with a control increases, the need for the auditor to perform his or her own work on the control increases

- Use a top-down approach
  - Begin at the financial statement level with the auditor's understanding of the overall risks to internal control over financial reporting
    - Does management's philosophy and operating style promote effective internal control over financial reporting?

Reporting on Internal Control in an Integrated Audit (continued)

- Does management have sound integrity and ethical values?
- Does the Board or audit committee understand and exercise oversight responsibility over financial reporting and internal control?

- Then focus on entity-level controls
  - Especially controls over management override

- Then focus on significant accounts and disclosures and their relevant assertions depending on
  - Size and composition of the account
  - Susceptibility to misstatement due to errors or fraud
  - Volume of activity or complexity of the individual transactions
  - Nature of the account or disclosure
  - Accounting and reporting complexities associated with the account

Reporting on Internal Control in an Integrated Audit (continued)

- Exposure to losses in the account
- Possibility of significant contingent liabilities
- Existence of related-party transactions in the account
- Changes from the prior period in account or disclosure characteristics

- Understanding likely sources of misstatement: auditor should
  - Understand flow of transactions related to the relevant assertions
  - Identify the points within the company's processes at which a material misstatement could arise
  - Identify the controls that management has implemented to address these potential misstatements
  - Identify the controls that management has implemented over unauthorized use of the company's assets that could result in a material misstatement

Reporting on Internal Control in an Integrated Audit (continued)

- Perform walk-throughs
  - Follow a transaction from origination through the company's processes until it is reflected in the company's financial records
- **The auditor's report** on the audit of internal control over financial reporting must include a title with the word "independent" and
- Must include following statements
  - Management is responsible for maintaining and assessing effective internal control over financial reporting
  - The auditor's responsibility is to express an opinion on the company's internal control over financial reporting

Reporting on Internal Control in an Integrated Audit (continued)

- Definition of internal control
- The audit is in accordance with GAAS
- The auditor is required to plan and perform the audit to obtain reasonable assurance about whether effective internal control over financial reporting was maintained in all material respects
- The auditor believes the audit evidence is sufficient and appropriate to provide a basis for the opinion
- Because of inherent limitations, internal control over financial reporting may not prevent or detect misstatements and projections of any evaluation of effectiveness to future periods are subject to risk
- The auditor's opinion on whether the company maintained, in all material respects, effective internal control over financial reporting as of the specified date

- The manual or printed signature of the auditor's firm

- The city and state of the auditor's office

- The date of the audit report

PCAOB Reporting on Whether Material Weaknesses Still Exist

- The auditor may report on whether previously reported material weaknesses (PRMW) exist if management
  - **Accepts** responsibility for the effectiveness of internal control
  - **Asserts** that the specific control(s) identified is effective
  - Supports the assertion with documented evidence
  - Provides a written report containing required elements

Employee Benefit Plans

- Audits of employee benefit plans (EBPs) include Employee Retirement Income Security Act of 1974 (ERISA) and Department of Labor requirements.

- EBPs include defined contribution plans (401k, 403b, ESOP) and defined benefit plans (traditional, cash balance).

- EBPs are unique in allowing limited scope audits when assets held by qualified, regulated financial institution.
  - Financial institution provides certification for investments and related investment activity.
  - Audit procedures **exclude** certified investment assets and activity.
  - Audit procedures performed on noninvestment activities of plan (e.g., employee and employer contributions, participant loans, administrative expenses).

Attestation Engagements—General

Subject matter and criteria always present for such engagements

Frequently a written assertion is available

Form

- Examinations
- Reviews
- Agreed-upon procedures

Attestation Standards

In attestation engagements, the accountant expresses an opinion, a conclusion, or findings about the reliability of subject matter or a written assertion of another party

Must comply with standards for attestation engagements

Requirements for all attestation engagements:

- Acceptance of engagement only with reasonable likelihood that it can be completed successfully
  - Appropriate subject matter
  - Suitable and available criteria
  - Evidence needed expected to be obtainable

Attestation Standards (continued)

- Practitioners
    - Exercise professional skepticism
    - Have adequate knowledge of subject area
    - Perform engagement in accordance with professional standards and legal and regulatory requirements
    - Exercise due professional care in performing engagement
    - Adequately document engagement
- Report
    - Opinion, conclusions, or findings expressed in written report

Financial Forecasts and Projections

An accountant may be associated with prospective financial statements

- Prospective financial statements are the representation of a responsible party
- They provide an entity's financial position, results of operations, and changes in financial position for a future period of time

Prospective financial statements may be forecasts or projections

- **Forecasts** are based on what is expected to occur under normal circumstances
- **Projections** are based on what is expected to occur given one or more hypothetical assumptions

Forecasts may be prepared for general or limited use, but projections may only be prepared for limited use

- Statements prepared for **general use** will be used by those who are not necessarily directly negotiating with the responsible party
- Statements prepared for **limited use** will be used exclusively by those who are directly negotiating with the responsible party

Examination Engagements

An examination of prospective financial statements involves

- Evaluating the preparation of the statements and the support underlying the assumptions
- Evaluating whether the presentation of the statements conforms to AICPA presentation guidelines

The accountant's standard report on an examination of prospective financial statements should include

- Identification of the prospective statements presented by the responsible party
- Indication that the examination was made in accordance with AICPA standards and a brief description of the nature of the examination
- The accountant's opinion as to presentation in conformity with AICPA guidelines and that the underlying assumptions provide a reasonable basis for the forecast or for the projection given the hypothetical assumptions

Examination Engagements (continued)

- A statement that the prospective results may not be achieved
- A statement that the accountant is not responsible for updating the report
- Limitations on the use of the statements if the presentation is a projection or a limited use forecast

Agreed-Upon Procedures Engagements

The accountant may apply agreed-upon procedures to prospective financial statements provided

- The accountant is independent
- The accountant and specified users agree upon the procedures
- The specified users take responsibility for the sufficiency of the procedures
- Use of the report is limited to the specified users

Pro Forma Financial Information

Pro forma financial statements are based on historical information

- They consider an event or transaction that had not occurred as of the financial statement date
- They are restated to provide the information as if the event or transaction had occurred

The accountant will perform procedures to provide assurance that management's assumptions and presentation are reasonable

The report will identify the financial statements from which the historical information is derived

Auditors may perform examinations or reviews

Management Discussion and Analysis

Ordinarily included in annual or quarterly reports.

Auditors may perform examinations or review of this information.

Compliance Attestation Engagements

Ordinarily relates to **compliance with laws, regulations, rules, contracts, and grants.**

Responsible party provides a written management assertion concerning compliance and auditors perform procedures to determine whether assertion is accurate.

Types of engagements

- Agreed-upon procedures
- Examinations

INDEX

Index